Suspects

A Play

Giles Cole

Samuel French - London
New York - Toronto - Hollywood

ISBN 0 573 01899 5

Please see page iv for further copyright information.

SUSPECTS

Originally presented by Present Productions Ltd in association with the Grand Theatre, Swansea on 15th August 1989, directed by John Frankau, designed by Alan Pickford and with the following cast: Roy Boyd, Emma Chambers, Gordon Honeycombe, Diana Kent and Ben Onwukwe

CHARACTERS

Ellen
Fisher
Goss
Tindall
Liz
Mike (non-speaking)

The action takes place in a flat in South London, over a period of four days in September

Time—the present

ACT I	SCENE 1	Friday. About 7 p.m.
	SCENE 2	Friday. Just after 10 p.m.
	SCENE 3	Saturday. About 2 p.m.
ACT II	SCENE 1	Sunday. Late morning
	SCENE 2	Monday. About 2 p.m.
	SCENE 3	Monday. A short while later

CHARACTERS

Ellen Early 20s, pretty, impressionable; perhaps a hint of a regional accent; a girl struggling to reconcile her instinctive feelings with the situation in which they have placed her.

Liz Late 30s or thereabouts, has a sophistication and poise which Ellen cannot match, allied with a ruthless charm. She is enormously resourceful and enjoys a sense of danger.

Tindall Mid-40s, a man out of sorts with himself. He is good at his job but no longer derives any great sense of satisfaction from it; by no means a conventional policeman, there are question marks over both his methods and his track record.

Goss Early 30s, Tindall's sergeant, and much more "by the book" in his attitudes. A thoroughly decent chap, he is a constant foil for Tindall, whose manner and style he finds disconcerting (as indeed they are intended to be).

Fisher Early 40s, on the surface smooth-talking and courteous, but there is an ice-cool subtlety lurking just below it; self-assured, smartly dressed and therefore attractive, but not a man to tangle with lightly.

Mike A non-speaking part, but must be of similar age and physical build to Fisher.

Other titles by Giles Cole published by Samuel French Ltd:
Secrets (one act)

ACT I

Scene 1

The main action takes place in the living area of a purpose-built third floor flat near Clapham Common in South London, over a period of four days at the end of September

The flat is laid out in a comfortable but not altogether tasteful style. There are various houseplants, a stereo system and a small TV set. A number of very up-to-date posters and ornaments jostle for attention alongside more conventional furnishings

There are three doorways: one leading to the kitchen; one to the hall (by which there is a door intercom system); and one from the hall into the bedroom. A section of both bedroom and kitchen should be visible. There is a large sash window upstage, which overlooks the rear courtyard

Occasionally, the sounds of a train can be heard in the distance, and the hum of traffic on the main road in the other direction

Friday evening, about 7 p.m. The light is just beginning to fade

The sash window is wide open and there are no lights on in the flat. There are a few bundled up dust-sheets in evidence, plus a large tin of gloss paint

The lift is heard, then the front door of the flat opens, off, and Ellen appears. She is followed into the room by Fisher who is wearing a suit and carrying a brief-case. Ellen switches on a couple of table lamps, takes off her jacket. Fisher surveys the living room

Ellen Sorry about the smell of paint. My husband has been decorating this afternoon.

Fisher Fine. No problem. Actually, I quite like the smell of new paint. It reminds me of when I was a boy: my grandfather was always painting the house when I went round for Sunday tea. Sponge cake and emulsion: that was the smell of Sunday.

Ellen smiles politely. She is on edge but trying not to show it

Mind you, I'm not sure if it was called emulsion paint then . . .

Ellen Would you like a drink?

Fisher No, thank you.

Ellen Oh, please. Do have one. I'm going to. I hate drinking on my own . . .

Fisher Well. A small Scotch then. Just to keep you company.

Ellen Right. (*She proceeds to pour two drinks, her back towards Fisher*)

Fisher Anyway . . . my grandfather retired early, you see. I think he had to keep painting the house for something to do. The décor would change from week to week. Well. It seemed like that. It was quite a family joke . . .

Ellen Would you like ice, or soda or something?

Fisher No thanks.

Ellen adds ginger ale to her glass

Ellen Well, here you are then. (*Giving Fisher his glass*) Cheers.

Fisher Cheers.

Ellen sips her drink. Fisher raises his glass, but before drinking he notices one of the pictures on the wall. In contrast to some of the other more abstract or photographic prints, it is a conventional reproduction

I know that picture. Yes. It's a Monet, isn't it?

Ellen No, it's a print . . .

Fisher Yes, I realize that. I mean, if you had the original of that you'd hardly be living in a flat like this—oh, no offence, of course.

Ellen It was a present from my mother.

Fisher Very nice. (*He blows his nose*) Excuse me. Damn sniffles . . .

Ellen Do sit down, Mr Fisher.

Fisher Thank you.

They both sit. At about this point we become aware of a shadowy figure (Mike) sitting, very still, in the bedroom

Ellen Well, cheerio then. (*She sips her drink*)

Fisher also drinks, then takes out his handkerchief and wipes his nose

Fisher Mrs Stacey, would you mind if I closed the window a fraction? Seems a bit chilly now the evenings are drawing in . . .

Ellen Oh. Erm . . .

Fisher And I don't want to get any more of a cold than I've already got, do I?

Ellen No. Well, the paint will still be a bit wet, you see . . .

Fisher Ah.

Ellen That's really why it's open.

Fisher Yes, of course . . .

Ellen I could put the heating on. It's about time we switched it back on again anyway.

Fisher No, don't trouble. I'll check the window. (*He carefully touches the raised sash*) Seems okay on the top here . . . (*He tries to slide the sash down. It shifts slightly but stays put*)

Ellen (*agitated*) Please, I really think you ought to leave it . . . My husband wouldn't be very pleased if you . . .

Fisher No, quite. Will he be long, do you think?

Ellen Oh no. (*She doesn't elaborate*)

Fisher Just washing out his paint-brush, is he?

Ellen Erm, I don't think he bothers, actually. I think he just sticks it in a jar of water.

Fisher I see . . . You are sure, Mrs Stacey, that he will want to talk to me?

Ellen Oh yes! He'll be delighted. It's exactly what he's been going on about recently—savings plans, and personal equi-thingies or whatever they're called ... He was saying how he'd like to know more about them.

Fisher I take it you do already have life insurance?

Ellen Oh yes. Well, I think so. I'm not entirely sure, to be honest. My husband deals with all that, you see ...

Fisher Mm. Well, as I said, we also offer advice on pension schemes, school fee plans, medical insurance ... (*He snaps open his briefcase and pulls out a wodge of papers*)

Ellen I think you'd better tell him all about it, Mr Fisher.

Fisher Alan, please ...

Ellen Quite funny really, isn't it? Alan and Ellen ...

Fisher Just a vowel between us, you might say.

Ellen smiles politely. This is proving more difficult than she thought. Fisher sips his drink, again dabs at his nose

Do you often find yourself in Chippendales, Ellen?

Ellen No, not really. I just happened to be, you know, passing.

Fisher Ah.

Ellen I popped in once before with my friend Jean, as a matter of fact. Just by chance—you know.

Fisher I'm quite a regular. I usually have a glass or two on a Friday after work.

Ellen It's ... very nice. Very civilized.

Fisher Oh, it is. It's definitely got a bit of class, which isn't always the case in Clapham. Have you lived here long?

Ellen Oh, quite a while, yes. Almost a year now.

Fisher I take it you led a fairly nomadic existence beforehand ...

Ellen (*not understanding*) Erm, no. Not really ... I worked in a shop in Peterborough.

Fisher Ah yes. Peterborough. (*Pause*) Yes, they do a pretty decent house white in Chippendales.

Ellen (*beginning to lose her nerve*) Look, I'm sorry to keep you waiting, Mr F ... Alan. I'd better go and see if I can find him. He ... may have got cornered by Mrs Richards. The lady on the ground floor ...

Fisher You do that, Ellen.

Ellen Yes. Right ...

Ellen exits through the hall

Fisher goes to the drinks, checks the whisky bottle, then starts looking around the room. He goes over to the window, checks the amount of whisky still in his glass, turns and looks out of the window

He goes to the kitchen, glances round it, then strolls over to the bedroom. If we haven't noticed the figure in the bedroom before, we do now—not clearly enough to distinguish features, but enough to see Mike rise and move stealthily to behind the door

Fisher opens the door, slowly, peers in, switches on the light. The room is apparently empty. He switches off the light, closes the door again

Mike remains motionless

Ellen enters, a little out of breath. Fisher whirls round to face her

Fisher Sorry. I was miles away. You made me jump.

Ellen looks at him for a moment, as if divining his intentions

Ellen Yes, he was downstairs. I told him I'd met you, and that I was sure he'd like to have a chat with you, and so on . . . He said to give you a drink . . . Said he'd be up in a second.
Fisher Fine.
Ellen I am sorry about this . . . I expect your wife will be wondering where you are.
Fisher I doubt it. My wife is in North Wales with her lover.
Ellen Oh, I'm . . .
Fisher He's a maintenance man on the Snowdonia Mountain Railway. Half her age. It's odd, really. She's always hated trains. Still . . . they seem to rub along together. How about you? Do you like trains?
Ellen Erm . . . yes, I suppose. I haven't ever really thought about it . . . Can I get you another drink then?
Fisher Why not? What the hell. You only live once.

Ellen fills Fisher's glass again with her back to him. He smiles to himself, checks his watch

Ellen Here you are.
Fisher You're very kind.
Ellen Not at all. (*She turns to fill her glass*)

Small pause

Fisher There's no husband, Ellen, is there?
Ellen I beg your pardon?
Fisher All this—it's a charade, isn't it?
Ellen (*nervously*) I don't know what you mean . . .
Fisher Oh come on. An attractive girl on her own in a wine bar—gets chatting to a man—invites him back to her flat, supposedly to talk to her husband about financial matters, plies him with drink . . . and lo and behold, no hubby. I'm not stupid, Ellen. And I really don't think you are either, so don't insult yourself. Please. Let's just be honest about it . . . (*He puts down his glass, and approaches her*) We all get lonely, Ellen. I understand that only too well.
Ellen (*edging away*) No. No. Please . . .
Fisher Okay, okay. You don't want to rush things. I can understand that too. You don't want me to get the wrong impression.
Ellen It's not that . . .
Fisher Perhaps you just want to talk. That's okay too. I'm not a monster, Ellen. I'm not going to assault you. (*Brief pause*) I can't stand those

bastards who force themselves on women, sometimes at knifepoint too . . . To me that's barbaric. I couldn't do anything like that. Come and sit down. (*He sits on the sofa, in front of the open window*)

Ellen looks at him, considers, then she also sits, but not too close to him

Perhaps your husband's away on business . . . Perhaps you don't have a husband at all . . . It makes no odds, Ellen. We can just sit and relax and enjoy each other's company. Like civilized human beings.

Ellen Yes . . .

Fisher You see, that's better, isn't it?

Ellen Yes . . . (*She gives an involuntary shiver*)

Fisher Bit of a nip in the air tonight . . . Autumn is most definitely upon us.

Ellen (*smiling*) You haven't touched your drink.

Fisher Oh, I've been knocking it back all right . . . (*We haven't noticed him drink; but he does now, then seems about to sneeze. He extracts the handkerchief, and the sneeze subsides*) False alarm. Sorry.

Ellen I suppose you meet a lot of women on their own, do you, in your line of work?

Fisher Very few, as a matter of fact. No, I'll amend that statement: very few under the age of three score and ten. (*He slides closer to her*) I don't suppose there's such a thing as a curtain about the place, is there?

Ellen What?

Fisher Only we do seem to be rather exposed to public view here . . .

Ellen I can't put the curtains back until the paint's dry. But don't worry. No-one can see in. This is the back of the building, you see. The next block of flats is over that way. (*She points*)

Fisher (*moving towards the bedroom*) How about in that room? What's the curtain situation in there?

Ellen No! No. Please. Let's stay here. Please.

Fisher As you wish . . .

Fisher smiles. He touches Ellen's hair, and kisses her lightly. She doesn't push him away. He leads her to the sofa, kisses her again, more fully. They hold this position for a few seconds, then Fisher slides gently sideways

Ellen At last . . .

Fisher is draped over the sofa. Ellen extricates herself and shudders. She grabs her jacket and hurries into the bedroom

Mike . . . the drink's worked at last . . . He's unconscious. I'll leave you to it . . . OK?

Ellen kisses Mike

Ellen exits

Mike emerges from the bedroom, still an indistinct figure, and appears in the hall doorway. We can just discern a cudgel-shaped weapon in his hand. He starts to move towards Fisher

Black-out

Scene 2

The same evening, just after 10 p.m.

The room is as before and there is no-one to be seen

Ellen enters slowly from the hall, blank-faced, lost

Goss appears at her side, switching on the main lights, and guiding her to the sofa. She is hardly aware of his presence. She sits

Goss I'm very sorry, Mrs Stacey. But we have to be certain . . .

Ellen nods

Look, we . . . we can leave this for the moment if you prefer, but I do need to ask a few questions . . . First of all, can you tell me what time you went out this evening?

Ellen (*softly*) Erm . . . about half past seven, I think . . .

Goss I beg your pardon?

Ellen About half past seven . . .

Goss And your husband, Mike, was here when you left?

Ellen Yes. He was decorating. He wanted to finish before it got dark . . .

Tindall enters briskly from the hall

Ellen and Goss both turn to look at Tindall

Tindall motions Goss to leave the room

Slight pause

Goss exits

Tindall looks at Ellen for a moment, and adopts a sympathetic tone

Tindall Mrs Stacey . . . I know you've had a severe shock, and I'm sorry to ask you this, but had your husband's behaviour been in any way different recently?

Ellen What?

Tindall Had he seemed at all upset by anything? Disturbed?

Ellen No . . . Why?

Tindall Had anything unusual happened?

Ellen I don't understand what you're getting at!

Tindall Where did you go this evening, Mrs Stacey?

Ellen I . . . I went to see Jean . . .

Tindall Jean?

Ellen A friend of mine. Jean Heywood. She lives on the other side of the Common . . .

Tindall Were you with her all evening?

Ellen Yes. We went for a pizza. We were going to go to the cinema but we got the times wrong. Jean can't stand going into a film after it's started, so we went for a pizza instead . . .

Goss enters

Tindall I see. Well, thank you, Mrs Stacey. You've been very patient. Now——

Ellen (*distressed*) I think I'd like to go and lie down. I feel dizzy ...

Tindall Of course.

Goss holds the door for Ellen who goes through into the bedroom, in a daze. Tindall watches her, a touch longer than necessary, then turns

What is it, Gossy?

Goss There's a lady outside.

Tindall Yes?

Goss A visitor. Just arrived. Says she's Mrs Stacey.

Tindall Does she now? Mr Stacey's mother, would you say?

Goss Not unless she's had half a dozen facelifts and a body transplant.

Tindall Well well. (*He goes to close the window, carefully using the sash lifts. It moves freely enough, but the paintwork is still tacky*)

Goss Wet paint, sir.

Tindall (*giving a withering look*) Thank you, Sergeant.

Goss Or tacky, to be more exact. Been drying two or three hours, I'd say.

Tindall DIY expert, are you?

Goss I do my bit around the house.

Tindall Keep it nice for your little wife ...

Goss (*used to this*) Yeh, yeh ... Fetch her in, shall I, sir?

Tindall Bring your wife with you now, do you? That's taking marital harmony a bit far ...

Goss (*patiently*) I told Mrs Stacey to wait by the lift ...

Tindall Yes, fetch her in, Gossy. Let's see if we can make some sense of all this.

Goss exits into the hall

Tindall scans the room, spots the tin of paint by the back wall, near the window. Using a handkerchief, he lifts it carefully, checks it and its position in relation to the window, then replaces it

Liz enters, followed by Goss

Liz Please, can somebody tell me what is going on here?

Tindall (*scanning the room*) I am Detective Inspector Tindall; this is Detective Sergeant Goss. (*He produces his warrant card*) C.I.D. And who might you be?

Liz There's no "might" about it. I *am* Liz Stacey.

Tindall gives her an inquiring look

Mike Stacey is my ex-husband.

Tindall I see. (*He continues his inspection*)

Goss Everything has been checked, sir ...

Tindall Not by me, Sergeant.

Liz Look, I presume there's been some kind of accident——

Tindall Let me just get this straight. You are divorced from Mr Stacey, yet you remain on friendly terms with him and his present wife, to the extent, at any rate, that you call round to visit, on an off-chance, at . . . ten, ten-fifteen, in the evening?

Liz Is that so odd?

Tindall It's interesting.

Liz You obviously have a very old-fashioned view of marital relationships, Inspector.

Tindall Perhaps so, perhaps so . . .

Liz Now will you please tell me what's happened!

Tindall Sergeant . . .

Tindall gestures to Liz to sit, then perseveres with his examination: there are, for instance, various ornaments, a few magazines, an ashtray full of cigarette stubs

Goss At eight-thirty this evening we received a report of a man lying unconscious in the yard at the rear of this block of flats. The nearest available beat officer called an ambulance at approximately eight thirty-five. (*He refers to his notebook*) The man's clothing was paint-stained and there was a paint-brush lying a few feet away, suggesting that he had fallen—from this window—whilst decorating.

Liz Oh my God . . .

Goss The man has been identified as Michael Dennis Stacey. It . . . um, only remains to say that in the opinion of the Divisional Surgeon death would have been instantaneous.

Liz rises abruptly, moves away, stops, turns. She looks at them, gives a disbelieving gasp, then moves away again

Tindall makes as if to guide her back to her chair

I wouldn't, Jack, if I were you. Best not to interrupt the natural momentum . . .

Tindall again looks witheringly at Goss, but desists

It sometimes helps to disperse the inner tension in times of crisis and stress.

Tindall Is that so?

Goss Just a theory of mine. Other people go stock still, barely breathing.

Tindall Gossy, shut up and get the lady a drink.

Goss, hurt, goes to the drinks trolley, and pours a brandy. Liz stops pacing during this exchange

Liz I can't believe this . . . I just can't believe it can have happened—I realize that must be the obvious thing to say, but . . . I'm sorry, it's just too . . . I don't know . . . (*She can't find the words*)

Goss, sympathizing, hands her the glass. Liz takes it, drinks

Are you certain? I mean, are you absolutely certain? Yes, of course you are—what a stupid question. Oh my God—Ellen. Where is she? Was she here when it happened?

Tindall No.
Goss She got back about half an hour ago.
Liz She knows then?
Goss Yes. She knows. She has just identified the body.
Liz Oh, poor girl . . . They haven't been married very long either . . . Well, thank God she didn't find him, that's one mercy.
Tindall What makes you say that?
Liz What?
Tindall That Mrs Stacey—that is to say, the present Mrs Stacey—didn't find her husband's body.
Liz Well, I . . . I assumed from what you said—about an ambulance being called, and Ellen not being here when it happened . . .
Tindall Assumptions can be misleading.
Liz What's that supposed to mean?

Goss retrieves Liz's glass

Goss Mr Tindall enjoys being cryptic, Mrs Stacey. It's just his manner. Please don't concern yourself.
Liz You two are weird, you know that? Weird.

Ellen enters from the bedroom

Ellen (*seeing Liz*) Oh . . .
Liz Ellen——
Ellen What are you doing here?
Liz Well, I called round. As I said I might, after my appointment this evening . . . I brought you these brochures . . .

Liz takes a couple of holiday brochures from her bag. Ellen stares at her. Not knowing what to do with them, Liz puts them back in her bag. There is a brief but distinctly awkward pause

Oh Ellen, I don't know what to say . . . I'm so sorry . . . What a terrible, terrible thing . . .

Ellen continues to look at her with a blank, numb expression

If there's anything I can do . . . I know everyone always says that, but I mean it. Really. Just ask.

Tindall, upon whom none of the foregoing has been lost, finds a sheet of printed paper under the sofa. He hands it to Goss

Goss Is this relevant?
Tindall Everything is relevant, until I decide otherwise. You know that. (*He goes to re-check the window*)
Liz Come and sit down, Ellen. Do you want to talk? To talk about it?
Ellen Erm . . . Yes . . . No . . . I don't know. Liz . . .
Tindall Anything else, anywhere, of any *relevance*, Sergeant?
Goss No, sir. Well, just a paint-brush in the kitchen.
Tindall Yes?

Goss Three-quarter inch, I'd say. Soaking in an old cup. (*In a confidential tone*) Looks like the same paint as on the brush outside.
Tindall How very surprising.
Goss That was a two-inch brush.
Tindall (*ironically*) Thank you.

Suddenly Ellen starts to shake and emit little involuntary yelps or moans as she tries to control herself. Liz puts an arm round her

Liz That's right. Let it out. Good girl . . .
Goss Have we finished here for the time being, Jack? Only I think . . .

Goss nods in the direction of Liz and Ellen

Tindall Yes . . . (*He motions Goss to leave*)

Goss exits

(*To Liz*) *You're* not planning any trips abroad for the time being, are you, Mrs . . . er . . .?
Liz (*irritated at his continued intrusion*) Stacey. No. Not for the time being.
Tindall Only we may need to talk to you again.
Liz Fine.
Tindall I think it would be a good idea if somebody could stay with her. Are there any friends nearby? Apart from Jean Heywood, that is.
Liz I'll stay.
Tindall Well, if you're sure you're the best person——
Liz Don't worry, Inspector. We can look after each other.
Tindall As you wish. Good night, Mrs . . .
Liz Oh, for goodness' sake call me Liz. If it makes things easier for you.
Tindall Right. Liz it is then. Right . . . (*He looks appraisingly at them both for an instant*) I'll be in touch.

Tindall exits

The front door closes (off)

Liz remains momentarily with her arm round Ellen, who is now beginning to calm down. Liz then detaches herself, checks in the hall that both men have gone. We hear the lift. Satisfied, she takes off her coat. Her manner now changes abruptly

Liz All right, Ellen. You can stop acting now.
Ellen (*looking up, tearfully*) What?
Liz (*helping herself to another drink*) It's all very fetching, but, please, spare me the encores.

Ellen stares at her in amazement and disbelief

Ellen How can you . . .?
Liz Yes, very good, very good, but don't get carried away on my behalf. I'm not an appreciative audience. (*She pours a second drink*)
Ellen I . . . don't understand what you're saying . . . I thought we, you know . . . I thought we got on.

Liz Oh we do, we do. I'm very fond of you, Ellen dear. You're like the younger sister I never had. We have an affinity.

Ellen What?

Liz Have a drink.

Ellen (*taking it*) Liz, why are you being like this? I don't know what you're talking about . . .

Liz This elaborate grief . . . I could believe in it a little more if I felt it was occasioned by the right person—namely, the man we both love to hate, your husband and mine, Mr Mike laugh-a-minute Stacey. But, dear Ellen, what you are reckoning without is the fact that I too have seen the body.

Ellen Seen him? When?

Liz Ten-fifteen is rather late to call by—even to visit two old chums like you and Mike—as the Inspector so readily spotted. What I failed to point out is that I called earlier as well, at about a quarter to eight. There was no answer on the entry-phone downstairs, so I went round the back to see if there were any lights on up here. I thought the old bastard might be ignoring the bell deliberately. I thought he might be in one of his churlish moods. Or perhaps you don't know about those yet . . . However, I didn't cast so much as one eye up to the dizzy heights of the third floor. No, my attention was grabbed by something much more at ground level . . .

Ellen Oh God . . .

Liz Yes, it gave me a hell of a jolt. Like you, I can't bear looking at a scratched finger let alone a complete corpse.

Ellen gives a little cry

It was lying, hunched up, near those great dustbin things. Oh, at a glance it looked like Mike—his clothes and so on, his sort of build—but you know, and I know, that it wasn't him.

Ellen You're mad, Liz. Mad . . .

Liz Mike and I may have finished over two years ago, but I can still recognize the old reprobate's body when I see it. And that wasn't it.

Ellen But it was dark, and his face was all . . .

Liz Oh, agreed. (*She smiles, drinks*) It's curious, isn't it, that things which would normally make you quite sick to look at them can sometimes be strangely fascinating. It's like people gawping at road accidents, I imagine.

Ellen Look, Liz, if this is some kind of nasty game . . . Some sort of . . .

Liz What? Some sort of what?

Ellen I don't know, but whatever it is, it's in very bad taste . . .

Liz laughs at her

Oh, stop it! Stop it!

Liz takes out the holiday brochures, and starts to flick through them

Liz You know, I've always fancied the Far East. Singapore. Hong Kong. Bali. Now Mike is more your Costa del Sol merchant. Cheap and cheerful and full of other sweaty Englishmen. Unless you've managed to cultivate him to some extent, which by the look of this flat I doubt. I tried, of course. But there are some battles one is doomed to lose. Mike's a sweetie in many ways, but impervious to the higher things in life, don't you find? Not to put too fine a point on it, he's a slob. Oh, in the nicest possible sense, naturally. I became quite fond of his beer gut eventually.

Ellen nervously lights a cigarette

I thought you'd given up smoking.

Ellen Look, if this is your way of trying to console me, thank you very much, but I'd rather you didn't bother. Now, if you don't mind, I think I'll go and have a bath . . .

Liz All right, have it your own way.

Ellen Whose body could it possibly have been if not Mike's?

Liz I thought you might be able to tell me that.

Ellen Liz, when I left this flat this evening Mike was here, decorating. He was doing the outside of the window. I told him to be careful for heaven's sake! Then I get back and the place is swarming with police . . . Apparently somebody—probably Mrs Richards from downstairs, she's always poking her nose in—apparently somebody rang them when they saw a dog, you know, sniffing around and barking . . . Oh God . . . Look, everything is ghastly enough without you . . . imagining things! He's such a bloody fool, he probably had a few Scotches, then got out on the window-ledge and lost his balance. And for all I know you're probably in some kind of alcoholic stupor yourself . . .

Liz (*putting down her glass*) Do I look drunk? Do I? Am I bumping into things, slurring my words—do I have a glazed look on my face?

Ellen You know very well you never get like that when you're drunk. That's what's so . . . off-putting about you. At least with Mike you knew when he'd had a few: there was no mistaking it. It was the one thing I didn't like about his relationship with you——

Liz Only the one thing? Surely not.

Ellen (*ignoring this*) You encouraged his drinking!

Liz Oh, did I, little Miss Purity?

Ellen Liz, for God's sake . . . Mike is *dead.* And we're carrying on as if he'd, you know, gone out for a packet of cigarettes or something.

Liz What are you up to, Ellen? Hm?

Ellen Liz, please, I can't take any more of this . . .

Liz I think I've underestimated you. I always thought you were a nice bright little thing, but a bit vacuous, do you know what I mean?

Ellen grinds out her cigarette

Now, though, something tells me you're being one clever little cookie. Otherwise, how on earth could you persist in believing that that bag of broken bones is your husband?

Ellen Liz, I *saw* him . . . They took me to the hospital . . .

Liz There'll be a post mortem, of course. And almost certainly an inquest. A violent death in suspicious circumstances . . .

Ellen What's suspicious about it?

Liz Oh, the calculated innocence of the girl. I love it, I just love it.

Ellen Please go, Liz.

Liz Why do you insist your husband's dead, Ellen? Mike never did a day's decorating in his life. Show him a paint-brush and he'd run a mile.

Pause

Don't you underestimate *me*, Ellen . . .

Ellen Why do you have to interfere in our lives? We just wanted to be left alone—to be happy. But you wouldn't ever let go, would you? You always had to be there. Why? Are you jealous or something? Jealous because he preferred me?

Liz Mike and I split up, finally, well before he met you, my dear. As you well know.

Ellen You could have anybody you want—why do you have to hang around here?

Liz Just because a marriage ends it doesn't mean you can't still be friends. I'm good at being friends with people. I always have been. In fact I pride myself on it.

Ellen Oh, look, this is stupid. Just go, please. Or do you want me to call the police back?

Liz Ooh. Is that a threat? Rather a bold one, if I may say so, for someone on such shaky ground.

Ellen Go. Please. Get out. Leave me alone!

Liz All right, Ellen, I'll go. But remember—I know my husband. My . . . ex-husband. I lived with him for ten years, on and off. And when he's up to his tricks, my sixth sense tells me so. (*She picks up the brochures again*) By the way, do you still want these? Still planning a little hol? Or did you have something more long-term in mind? Tell you what, I'll leave them in case. Have a nice hot bath, relax, and get a good night's sleep. But for goodness' sake go easy on the sleeping pills: we don't want another corpse on our hands, do we?

Liz collects her coat and her bag. Ellen sits on the sofa

I mean it about being friends, Ellen. There is no reason for us to fight, none at all, never has been. You can always come and stay at my place, should the need arise. There's plenty of room since I got rid of that dreadful property developer . . . I think he regarded me as the sexual equivalent of an off-shore tax haven . . . Ah well. Such is love amongst the moneyed classes . . .

Ellen refuses to respond, or even to turn and look at Liz. Liz goes to her, and leans over the back of the sofa

You can brazen it out as long as you like, Ellen, but you may come unstuck with the Coroner, you know. Unless I, too, swear that the body is Mike's. A formal identification by not just one wife, but two—now that would back up your story no end, wouldn't it? Night night, Ellen dear. I'll pop in again tomorrow . . .

Liz exits

Ellen continues to stare blankly ahead

Black-out

Scene 3

About 2 p.m. the next day

Goss and Tindall are in the room. The dust-sheets have been removed and the window is closed. The television set is on—an old movie which Ellen has presumably been watching. We hear a little stilted dialogue, then Tindall changes channels with the remote control. The sounds of a race meeting break the genteel mood of the film

Goss (*disapprovingly*) Jack . . .
Tindall Just time to catch the two o'clock . . .
Goss Still doing the gee-gees? I thought you'd given them up.
Tindall I've cut down. I'm on two a day now . . .
Goss Once a gambler always a gambler, eh?
Tindall There's no need to sound so superior. What's your sport? Bloody basketball . . .

Goss smiles and lets it go. Seeing he is not to be goaded, Tindall turns to the TV set and concentrates on the race

Goss Do you think any more Mrs Staceys are going to turn up this time, or is that the lot?

Tindall gives no response

I mean, for all we know there might be a whole league of them, all getting on like a house on fire.
Tindall It's an intriguing scenario, Gossy. And, in my experience of women, by no means impossible.
Goss Ah well, we all know about your experience of women . . . (*He idly picks up a copy of "Cosmopolitan" or similar magazine*)
Tindall It's the job, old son. Attracts them like flies, but plays merry hell with anything long-term . . .
Goss Doesn't affect me that way.
Tindall No, your domestic bliss is positively inhuman. My trouble is I married too early and divorced too late. A lethal combination . . .

Tindall turns back to the TV set. Goss puts the magazine down, looks at his watch

Goss Why are you so sure this wasn't an accident, Jack?
Tindall Ssh. (*He watches the end of the race, then switches off the set*) Eight to one. Not bad.

Goss Look, she goes out, leaves hubby slapping on a coat of gloss ... It's getting dark, he wants to finish the job off ... He reaches up to get at the top sash rail, and bob's your uncle ...

Tindall (*unconvinced*) No, no.

Goss It's happened before!

Tindall goes to the window, opens it, and leans out

Tindall What's the drop from here, do you reckon? Forty feet?

Goss Yes, at least that. I mean, there's that basement area at the back here: that adds a good ten feet or so.

Tindall And you think it was a simple accident? Yes?

Goss It's the most likely thing. Everything points to it.

Tindall And what about the second paint-brush? The one soaking in the kitchen?

Goss What about it? Painting a window often requires brushes of different sizes.

Tindall And which part of the window, in your opinion, is most likely to have been painted with the smaller brush in the kitchen?

Goss Well ... the narrower bits.

Tindall Quite so. And which parts of the window were most *recently* painted?

Goss Sorry, I don't follow.

Tindall The paint was still tacky, as you so skilfully pointed out, but some narrower bits were much tackier than the rest.

Goss looks blank

Which suggests, Sergeant, that somebody else painted those bits *after* Mike Stacey's death. Unless, of course, there is a way in which a man can plunge fifty feet into a courtyard, come back up again, and put his brush in to soak.

Goss Well, yes, all right. But they might have been tackier simply because he went over them again with the larger brush—you know, if he'd smudged them or something ...

Tindall And another thing. The can of paint was here, right? (*He indicates the position*)

Goss Yes ...

Tindall twists round, sits on the ledge, facing into the room

Tindall Then you explain to me how a man painting the outside of the window could possibly have reloaded his brush. (*He reaches towards the paint position*) He'd have needed arms at least two yards long!

Goss OK, OK. But the paint could've been moved! As evidence this is all pretty flimsy, Jack. I'm sorry, but it seems to me you're trying to turn this into something it's not.

Tindall You resent me, don't you, Gossy? (*He looks at the outside of the window again, still sitting on the ledge*)

Ellen enters from the bedroom, tidying her hair. She sees Tindall sitting there, as Mike must presumably have been sitting to paint the lower half of the window. She gives a gasp of horror

Tindall climbs back into the room

Sorry if I startled you.

Ellen It's just that . . . Seeing you sitting there . . .

Tindall Quite so, quite so. (*He closes the window*)

Tindall and Goss exchange glances. Goss is not impressed

Ellen (*collecting herself*) I'm . . . sorry I wasn't dressed when you arrived. I . . . Well, the truth is, I didn't actually go to bed till very late . . . I couldn't sleep, and . . . (*She gestures vaguely*)

Goss We quite understand, madam.

Ellen Oh God, I should've offered you a cup of tea or something——

Tindall Not necessary, I assure you.

A moment's pause. Ellen sits

Goss But thank you all the same.

Goss eyes Tindall again, who indicates, somewhat tetchily, that Goss should get on with the business in hand

Mrs Stacey, we've been checking a few details: your friend Miss Heywood has confirmed that you were with her from about a quarter to eight until twenty past nine, but her view was that your evenings together were hardly a regular routine . . .

Ellen Oh?

Goss A couple of Fridays in the last five weeks, but prior to that, nothing.

Ellen Well, we did lose touch a bit, I suppose, when I got married . . .

Tindall Not exactly bosom buddies, though, really, are you? A casual acquaintance from an abandoned typing course suddenly renewed five weeks ago . . .

Ellen What's wrong with that?

Tindall How long have you been married, Mrs Stacey?

Ellen Nearly a year.

Goss And would you describe it as a happy marriage?

Ellen Look, my husband did not commit suicide!

Small pause

I'm sorry. Yes. I would describe it as a happy marriage. Very happy.

Tindall Now, about the question of your husband's life insurance . . .

Ellen Oh, for God's sake! You really don't care, you lot, do you? You haven't got any . . . Oh, what's the word . . . for my feelings at all, have you? You just come blundering in here without any kind of by your leave, or . . . (*She turns away, distressed*)

Goss Mrs Stacey . . .

Tindall motions to Goss not to placate her, and he continues, in a level tone

Tindall I'm sorry if this appears brutal, Mrs Stacey, but you do understand, don't you, that the insurance company will want to make a few enquiries of their own?

Ellen (*angrily*) I hadn't really thought about it.

Tindall Customary procedure in a case like this.
Ellen Is it? Is it really?
Tindall Your husband used to work for an insurance company, I believe . . .
Ellen What of it?
Tindall Could you tell us when that was?
Ellen Before I met him. (*Short pause*) About four years ago—I think.
Goss What, that he *finished* working for them, you mean?
Ellen Yes. Look, I'm sorry, but I don't see what this has to do with . . . with my husband's . . . (*She can't bring herself to say the word*)
Tindall A hundred and seventy thousand pounds. That's what I believe his policy is worth. Is that accurate, would you say?
Ellen I really have no idea. He dealt with all that sort of thing. We didn't talk about it.
Tindall Never?
Ellen Not that I can remember. Look, Inspector——
Tindall Would you say you knew your husband well, Mrs Stacey?
Ellen What kind of a question is that?
Tindall Did you know, for instance, that he had a criminal record?
Ellen *What?*
Tindall Petty larceny. Nineteen seventy-one. Suspended sentence.
Ellen Larceny?
Goss He broke into a couple of cars.
Ellen No, I . . . Well, that's a long time ago . . .
Tindall In nineteen eighty, he was suspected of being involved in a drugs racket in West London. Cocaine and heroin. Know anything about that?
Ellen No . . . no . . . you're wrong. You're making this up . . .
Goss No charges were brought. Other suspects were arrested and enquiries regarding your husband were not pursued.
Ellen Well, there you are then!
Tindall In nineteen eighty-five, several thousand pounds' worth of funds were discovered to have been misappropriated from your husband's company.
Ellen So?
Tindall It smells, Mrs Stacey. It has what we policemen call "a bad odour" about it.

The lift can be heard (off)

Goss There were one or two subsequent dismissals but the investigation itself was, apparently, inconclusive.
Ellen Well, that's just typical of you police, isn't it? You'll believe what the hell you want to believe just because it suits you! Doesn't matter about the evidence, oh no, you'll have it in for somebody just because you bloody well feel like it!

Pause. Ellen collects herself. Again Tindall waits, assesses the situation, and decides to be blunt

Tindall The thing is, Mrs Stacey, there's a possibility this could be a murder case.

Ellen No . . . no . . .
Goss Which is why we want to establish certain details as quickly as possible.
Ellen (*moving near the window*) Mike was never like that . . . involved in those things . . . He was a good man—nobody would want to murder him! (*Instinctively, she touches the window then remembers and turns away*)
Tindall But have you ever had any reason to believe that your husband was being threatened in any way? Or blackmailed?
Ellen No!

The hall door swings open

There is a split-second pause

Liz enters carrying two bags of shopping

Goss assists Liz

Tindall Ah, the other Mrs Stacey. I didn't hear you arrive.
Liz I have my own key.
Tindall Well well.
Ellen Liz, tell them to go away! Tell them to leave me alone——
Liz All right, Ellen dear. Don't let them upset you . . .

Ellen sits, gently rocking herself

Mr Tindall, I really think you're being rather insensitive. This poor girl is beside herself with grief and worry. The strong-arm tactics can wait, surely?
Ellen They said Mike was a crook . . .
Liz Look, why don't you go and have a lie down, Ellen, and I'll bring you a cup of tea.
Tindall That's all right. Sergeant Goss will do it.
Goss Sir?
Tindall Off you go, Gossy. Tea.

Goss is far from happy about this instruction

Liz I got you some of those biscuits you like, Ellen. (*She hands them to Goss*) Custard creams. Do have one yourself, Sergeant.

Goss glowers and goes into the kitchen. Liz ushers Ellen towards the bedroom

Ellen (*worried*) What are you going to say to him? About Mike? What are you going to say?
Liz Why, nothing but the truth, of course.
Ellen The truth . . . yes . . .
Liz All I want, Ellen, is to have this whole dreadful business over and done with as soon as possible—for all our sakes.
Ellen Over and done with. Yes. But——
Liz (*hissing at Ellen*) Leave this to me.

Ellen goes into the bedroom

Liz returns, closing the bedroom door behind her. She removes her coat, hanging it over a chair

Now then, Inspector.

Tindall Now then, Mrs Stacey.

Liz Let's lay our cards on the table. You think Mike could have been murdered.

Tindall It's a strong possibility.

Liz In which case, your list of suspects would presumably include both myself and Ellen.

Tindall Correct.

Liz Then let me save you a lot of fuss and bother—it wasn't either of us.

Tindall How kind of you to tell me.

Liz I do so love helping the police.

Tindall You don't by any chance know who might have done it, do you?

Liz No. I don't.

Tindall smiles. Liz takes one bag of shopping to the kitchen

Tindall Well, that puts paid to that conversation, doesn't it?

Liz Actually, I doubt if anybody did murder him, but you seem the sort of man who likes to think the worst of everyone and everything.

Tindall Thank you.

Liz puts a few things into the fridge, leaving a pint of milk on top of it

Liz Milk, Sergeant . . .

Goss (*coming briefly into view*) Right . . .

Liz returns, briskly, to the living room

Liz Also, in case you hadn't noticed, neither Ellen nor I were here when it would have taken place, but I'm sure that won't stop you trying to get a conviction.

Tindall You think I play dirty, do you, Mrs Stacey?

Liz Let's just say I've heard about you, Mr Tindall.

Tindall Oh yes? Nothing good, I hope.

Liz You could have been a DCI by now. But you got a bit rough with somebody. Threw away your chances of promotion.

Tindall Did I now?

Liz Like you threw away your marriage. That strikes me as rather reckless, Inspector.

Tindall Who's the detective here, me or you?

Liz I like to know who I'm dealing with.

Tindall (*vaguely apprehensive*) Oh so do I, so do I . . .

Liz You don't remember me, do you?

Tindall Should I?

Liz A friend of mine is very pally with your Chief Superintendent. We met socially, once.

Tindall looks at her appraisingly, but says nothing

"Small world" is the expression I think you're looking for.

Tindall You must be mistaken. My Chief Super is not the sociable kind. He prefers golf.

Liz Sorry. I should have said ex-Chief Superintendent.

Tindall Ah. Well, that's a different matter.

Liz We had quite an evening of it. I'm surprised you don't remember. Mind you, you didn't stay long.

Tindall No, well, I'm not the sociable kind either.

Liz That was only too apparent. (*She starts to sort the other shopping bag. It mostly contains bottles of spirits and mixers*)

Tindall Why are you here, Mrs Stacey?

Liz Oh, please call me Liz. After all, we are almost old acquaintances . . .

Tindall Why are you here, *Liz*?

Liz Simple. I'm popping in to keep an eye on Ellen, do her shopping and so on. She doesn't have many friends, you know—at least not in London—and she's taking this very badly.

Tindall Whereas you, if I'm not much mistaken, are thriving on it. Why?

Liz Not thriving, Inspector. That's far too ungallant an interpretation. But I do take life as I find it.

Tindall And death too, presumably.

Liz In the midst of life, as the saying goes . . .

Tindall Are you really as cool a customer as you like to make out, Liz, or are you playing games with me?

Liz A little of each, I fancy.

Tindall That could get you into trouble.

Liz I like living dangerously.

Goss enters

Goss Cup of tea for anyone else while I'm at it?

Tindall (*pointedly*) No, thank you.

Goss Oh. Right then.

Goss exits into the kitchen

Tindall How come you kept in such close contact with your ex-husband?

Liz It wasn't exactly close. I met Ellen a few times, that's all. She's a nice girl. It was all very civilized.

Tindall Was Ellen responsible for the split between you and Mike Stacey?

Liz (*smiling*) No, no . . .

Tindall What did he do after he left the insurance firm?

Liz He toyed with the idea of running his own haulage business, but he couldn't raise the capital. Eventually he became a rep for a company supplying fitted kitchen units.

Tindall Not exactly high-powered then?

Liz Insurance was his game.

Tindall Yes. His life policy is pretty substantial, isn't it?

Liz He believed in his product. What's wrong with that?

Tindall I don't know, yet.

Liz So cynical and hard-bitten. Dear oh dear.

Goss enters with a teapot and cups, etc on a tray. He carries it, with elaborate care, to the bedroom, shooting a glance at Tindall, who ignores him

Tindall (*to Liz*) You've got enough stuff there for a fortnight. Are you planning a siege?
Liz Why? Are you offering to besiege me?
Tindall Not my department, I'm afraid . . .

Goss knocks on Ellen's door

Goss enters Ellen's room, leaves the tray, and waits, out of sight, in the hall

Ellen eventually pours herself a cup of tea

Why was Mike sacked from the insurance company?
Liz He resigned.
Tindall Call it what you will. Why?
Liz Principle.
Tindall Oh, they have those, do they, insurance salesmen?
Liz Now don't be snide, Mr Tindall. He resigned because he didn't see eye to eye with some new manager they brought in. He wasn't going to be dictated to by a man he didn't respect.
Tindall And this had nothing to do with the investigation into the firm's accounts?
Liz You have been quick off the mark, haven't you? No, it had nothing to do with it as far as I know.
Tindall What were your feelings when he declared his intention of marrying again?
Liz Oh, come on. You can do better than this. You suspect foul play, for some reason best known to yourself, and you fish around for a motive like a child with a shrimping net.

Liz puts the remainder of the contents of the shopping bag into the kitchen, re-emerging immediately

Tindall How about this hypothesis . . . With the connivance of his wife, Mike Stacey fakes his own death, in order to claim on the insurance and start a new life abroad, under an assumed name.
Liz (*laughing*) And why would he need to do that?
Tindall You tell me. Who knows what kind of pressures build up inside someone? Perhaps he couldn't stand the heat . . .
Liz Heat?
Tindall So he had to get out of the fitted kitchen . . .
Liz Oh, very droll.
Tindall Perhaps he had to disappear in a hurry . . . pay off a debt . . . Perhaps it was simply for the adventure of it all. Men can do peculiar things when they hit middle age—or so I'm told.
Liz That's true enough. But a murder plot, with *Ellen*? Somehow I don't see it, Inspector . . .
Tindall Call me Jack. You'd be surprised how many hare-brained schemes

people think up in an attempt to get rich quick. It's usually a combination of greed and desperation, in almost equal measures. It used to fascinate me at first, when I was a fresh young copper, but now ... now I leave the psychology to Sergeant Goss.

Liz (*smiling*) Talking of equal measures, would you care for one?

Tindall Maybe next time ... Oh, one other thing. Why didn't Mike get a job with another insurance company—if there was no disgrace, or misdemeanour, on his part?

Liz I suggest you ask all the insurance companies he applied to.

Tindall I see.

Liz His age may have been against him, of course. Now then, Inspector ... Jack ... Next time you intend delving into my private life, perhaps you could make it a less formal occasion ... (*She holds Tindall's gaze for a moment*)

Ellen, obviously anxious, enters from the bedroom

Oh, Ellen, I was just saying—insurance is a young man's game. Wouldn't you agree?

Ellen I don't know ... I've never really thought about it ...

Goss follows Ellen in from the hall

Tindall Gossy been looking after you, has he, Mrs Stacey? He makes a mean cup of tea. Very well trained is Sergeant Goss. And I don't just mean as a policeman.

Ellen Yes, he's ...

Tindall Well done, Sergeant.

Goss (*with forbearance*) Are we off now, sir?

Tindall We are. (*To Liz*) Perhaps I'll take you up on that less formal occasion ...

Liz By all means. (*She smiles*)

Tindall gives a nod of acknowledgement, duly noticed by Goss

Tindall (*to Ellen*) Thank you for your help, Mrs Stacey ... (*He heads for the hallway*) Come along, Gossy.

Goss We'll see ourselves out ...

Tindall and Goss exit

The front door closes (off)

Ellen immediately rounds on Liz

Ellen What have you been saying to him?

Liz They're not stupid, Ellen. They know something's up.

Ellen I just wish you'd keep out of this, Liz! I'm not a child, you know. I can look after myself!

Liz That remains to be seen. Oh, by the way, the shopping came to thirty-eight pounds. But don't worry—you can have it on account.

The lift is heard, off

Ellen What was all that about a less formal occasion?

Liz Mr Tindall and I are old friends. Isn't that lucky?

Ellen Old friends?

Liz Well, a slight exaggeration perhaps. A dear chum of mine used to know his former boss. This was when I was still married to Mike, of course. Though I didn't always let on about that . . .

Ellen Some wife you must have been.

Liz Now now, Ellen, don't be harsh with me. Mike and I were never the perfect couple, but we tolerated each other's little ways, and you can't say fairer than that.

Ellen You don't want to talk to Tindall any more than you have to, do you? I mean, it seems stupid——

Liz Talking to people is one of life's pleasures, Ellen. I know you can hardly string more than a dozen words together in any coherent fashion, but that is part of your charm . . .

Ellen Oh, thank *you.*

Liz Besides, Mr Tindall—Jack—is rather attractive, don't you find? Such interesting eyes . . .

Ellen You really can be a prize cow sometimes, can't you?

Liz Well, you know me, Ellen. I get bored so easily. It's my restless nature. Typical Pisces. Now, I'm off to spoil myself with a new outfit before the stores close. (*She collects her coat*) Have a nice afternoon. There's bound to be an old film on the box, or one of those frightful quiz shows you like so much.

She gives Ellen a quick kiss, and strokes her hair affectionately

See you later.

Liz exits

Ellen flicks through the TV channels, then suddenly freezes in panic

Ellen Oh my God! The time . . . (*She checks her watch, grabs the phone. She then opens a drawer and takes out a pocket calculator*) Now, what was it? Memory Recall . . . Yes . . . (*She presses a button, reads off the digits in the display, dials the number*) . . . 0 . . . 4 . . . 9 . . . 66. Right . . . Oh, come on, come on, be there, please . . . (*She waits an agonizing time for the phone to be answered*) Thank God. I thought I'd missed you . . . Oh, Mike, it's all going wrong. It's not going the way you said at all. I knew it wouldn't. I just knew it. Liz *knows.* She turned up last night, and saw the . . . saw him. And now she keeps going on at me—you know what she's like. I've got to see you, Mike. Please. I know you said not till . . . Mike? (*She looks at the receiver in her hand. A new panic sets in*) Who is that? (*She quickly replaces the receiver and gives a soft wail of both confusion and fear*)

Black-out

ACT II

Scene 1

Sunday. Mid-morning

Liz is re-hanging one of the curtains at the window with the aid of a stepladder. The other is already in position

Ellen is in the kitchen making coffee. She is wearing a dressing gown

Liz Well . . . I can't pretend that these revelations of yours are really a huge surprise. The only thing which *does* surprise me is that it's taken you until now to come clean. It is now Sunday: you have maintained your innocence, against overwhelming odds, for over thirty-six hours.
Ellen Well, I had to!
Liz To the police, yes. But not to me. I must design you some new curtains, Ellen, some nice swagged Austrian blinds or something. This flat could look very nice with a little effort . . . (*She comes down the ladder, and checks the curtains*)
Ellen I like it as it is . . .
Liz So. You laced Fisher's drink with Valium in order to speed up the effects of the alcohol. Very good. But why go to all that bother? Why didn't Mike just whack him over the head and have done with it?
Ellen Because he might have missed! Anyway, I'd've had to be there—to, you know, distract him—and I couldn't possibly have done that. Watched it. Not in a hundred years. (*She gives a shudder, and comes out of the kitchen with two mugs of coffee*)
Liz (*taking her coffee*) We all have to draw the line somewhere . . .
Ellen I thought we ought to just, you know, make him unconscious and then tip him out of the window, but Mike said we had to be quite sure he was, you know, dead. No use leaving him lying down there with a broken leg or something . . .
Liz Oh quite. Heaven forbid. This instant coffee is undrinkable, Ellen. I must get you some of my special Colombian blend.
Ellen I don't like proper coffee.
Liz No. Of course . . . (*Putting her mug down*) So, the deed being done, Mike then dressed in Fisher's clothes, I suppose, and left, in case anyone had seen Fisher arrive? (*She goes back up the ladder, and straightens the curtain*)
Ellen That's right.
Liz How very subtle. And this Mr Fisher was conveniently the same size as Mike, was he?
Ellen More or less. But Mike had checked that. Oh, Liz—I didn't want to

get involved in anything like this! But you know what he's like: it was either that or lose him altogether——

Liz A far safer option, I'd have thought.

Ellen But I love him, Liz! I'd do anything for him.

Liz Obviously. (*She comes down the ladder, and proceeds to put it away in the hall*) I feel sorry for you, I do really. A young girl with dreams of being a hostess on a TV game show ... all perfectly harmless, and silly ... You come to the ugly metropolis, and what happens? You immediately fall for an emotional gangster like Mike Stacey and lose what small sense of identity you already possessed.

Ellen I haven't lost my identity! I've just changed, that's all! I've grown up.

Liz laughs

(*Hurt*) Well, you can think what you like ...

Liz Thank you.

Ellen Anyway ...

Liz Hadn't you better get dressed, Ellen dear? It is nearly midday.

Ellen So what? (*Nevertheless she goes into the bedroom, and starts to pull on her clothes*)

Liz talks to Ellen via the open door

Liz And how do you imagine you'll feel, sitting in the sun on some Spanish island, wallowing in your new life, knowing you had to murder someone in order to get there?

Ellen Oh, don't, don't! Please. Don't go on about it!

Liz These things have to be faced, Ellen. It's a long-term business, murder.

Ellen Mike said it would pass, the feeling of, you know, guilt. Just being somewhere completely different would, like, make us different people. And eventually we'd forget.

Liz You believed that, did you?

Ellen Yes! Oh, look, it's all right for you, being so worldly-wise! You aren't the one who loves him!

Liz True. I no longer have that misfortune. Now, if, as you say, you lured poor Mr Fisher back here under false pretences, drugged him, and then left him to be despatched to the dustbin area by our dear husband while you and your pal Jean guzzled pizza Napoletana, how come no-one has missed him since early on Friday evening?

Ellen (*coming back into the living room*) Well, we knew he lived on his own now—so, what Mike's doing is dictating a telegram and sending it to Fisher's firm over the weekend, saying his mother's been taken ill abroad and that he's got to go and look after her ...

Liz And this telegram will therefore arrive first post tomorrow, before they have a chance to miss him?

Ellen That's right.

Liz And does he have a mother?

Ellen Yes, in Southampton. But she's away on a cruise with a friend of hers. That's why it all had to be now! Mike rang her up, as a salesman would, and asked for an appointment. She quite happily told him it was impossible because she was going away for several weeks.

Liz Silly woman.

Ellen I know. But there it is. Everything just seemed to fall into place. As if it was all *meant*.

Liz That is Mike talking.

Ellen (*with a faint smile*) Yes . . .

Liz And where, pray, is the devious old bastard now? Lying low somewhere?

Ellen (*nodding*) But that's the funny thing. He left me a number to ring him at, if I wanted to, and I did—ring him, I mean—but it was ages before he answered and then it wasn't him at all . . .

Liz Are you sure?

Ellen Well, no, not exactly. I mean, it was a bad line, and I admit I was in a bit of a state, but he hardly said anything to start with, and then he asked me who I was. Or whoever I was talking to did. I got really worried . . .

Liz Did he tell you where he was going to be?

Ellen No. He said it was safer not to.

Liz There you are then. He's staying in some boarding house somewhere, and the landlord answered. Or another guest. Did you ring again?

Ellen No, I didn't dare.

Liz Why not try again now? What's the number? (*She fetches the telephone*)

Ellen (*in an agony of indecision*) Oh, I don't know, Liz . . . He said to obey every instruction exactly . . . and . . . And I don't want to do anything stupid . . .

Liz There's ambition for you . . .

Suddenly Ellen gives a gasp

Ellen Oh my God . . .

Liz What? What is it?

Ellen I've just remembered—he said I had to erase the number!

Liz What are you talking about?

Ellen In the memory. On the calculator. (*She fetches it*) He said it was safer than writing it down, but I had to remember to erase it. And I didn't!

Liz Stop getting into such a tizzy, woman. Just dial the number. I'll speak to him if you like. No, on second thoughts best not to. I don't want to confuse the issue. Look, just ring him, Ellen. Then you can erase away to your heart's content.

Ellen No, but he obviously didn't *want* me to ring again, did he? (*She throws down the calculator, repeatedly runs her hands through her hair, in an attempt to stop them shaking*)

Liz Look, Ellen dear, you're obviously overwrought. I think the best thing you can do is lie down and rest, and I'll bring you another cup of instant bilgewater. Or something stronger if you prefer. Ellen?

Liz goes to Ellen, and takes hold of her. Ellen resists

Ellen, you must try to calm down . . . Look, I know how you must be feeling. You've suddenly realized you don't know whether you trust Mike any more, haven't you? It all seemed so remarkably simple and straightforward, and now it's all happening you're not quite so sure. About anything.

Ellen It's just that it's so . . . difficult, with no-one to . . . I just can't think straight . . . I don't know what to do!

Ellen is close to tears. Liz holds her, strokes her hair

Liz Come on now, don't upset yourself so much . . . I'm here. And I'll do whatever I can to help. We women have got to stick together, you know . . .

Ellen rummages in her bag for a hanky, taking out a couple of other things, one of which is a pill-box. Liz picks it up, looks at it, briefly

Oh, that's nice.

Ellen (*wiping her eyes*) Mike gave it to me. He said I mustn't let anyone know about it, but it might be useful if, you know, the worst came to the worst . . .

Liz (*picking the box up again*) Meaning?

Ellen Well, if the whole plan got screwed up, I suppose . . . Or I got arrested or something.

Liz I see . . . (*She opens it and sniffs the contents carefully*)

Ellen He said it was a strong sedative and it would knock me out, and then when I woke up I wouldn't remember what had happened . . .

Liz dabs a little finger into the box, which contains about a tablespoonful of white powder and tastes a tiny amount of it

Liz (*calmly*) I think I'd better look after this, Ellen. Don't you concern yourself with it.

Ellen Why? What is it?

Liz Well, there's no point in lying to you. It's pure unadulterated diamorphine. Or, in layman's terms, heroin. Probably from Iran, and, in a quantity like this, absolutely lethal.

Ellen How do you know?

Liz Believe me, I know. And at a rough guess, I'd say there's enough here to kill at least two people. Rather quickly. (*She removes her heavy silver bracelet and opens it out, revealing that it is, in effect, a hollow container. Expertly, she pours the powder into it, and puts the pill-box down*)

Ellen, meanwhile, is sitting in stupefied silence

So, if you'd taken this, you certainly wouldn't remember anything that happened. You wouldn't remember anything ever again. Are you beginning to understand your husband yet? (*She snaps the bracelet shut and replaces it on her wrist*) First Fisher, then you. Well, a massive overdose of heroin is *slightly* preferable to having your skull smashed in—I suppose. What did he use by the way? On Fisher?

Ellen is still staring, as if in a daze

The weapon, Ellen . . . What was it? Or, more to the point, where is it now?

Ellen It's . . . erm . . .

Liz Don't tell me it's still here . . .

Ellen nods

In this room?

Ellen Yes.

Liz Where, for God's sake? The police have been over the place with a fine tooth comb . . .

The intercom buzzes. They both freeze

You'd better answer it.

Ellen reluctantly answers the intercom

Ellen Hello? (*She gasps, covers the mouthpiece with her hand*) It's Tindall . . .

Liz Well, talk of the devil.

Ellen What are we going to do?

Liz You'd better let him in, hadn't you?

Ellen presses the button. Liz collects her bag etc.

And I think the best thing *I* can do is disappear . . .

Ellen What!

Liz It'll look suspicious if I'm here every time the police call.

Ellen No, Liz, you can't——

Liz Let's get one thing straight, Ellen, here and now. If you're to stand any chance of getting away with this extraordinary plan of yours, you'd better start doing as I say, and we'll discuss what *I* get out of it all later. After all, it looks as though I'm your only ally. Okay?

Ellen Well . . . yes, I suppose . . .

Liz You were always going to have to face the police alone at some stage, so you may as well start now. Don't worry. As far as they're concerned you've just lost your husband—they expect you to be jittery, for goodness' sake.

The lift is heard (off)

Ellen But why are they here *now*? On a Sunday?

Liz (*at the hall door*) They're trying to catch us off-guard. It's so obvious it's pathetic.

Ellen Liz!

Liz (*turning back*) What?

Ellen You can't get out now! They'll see you!

Liz I'm not going out. I'm going into the bedroom. Okay? If you can get rid of them, fine, but if you come unstuck I can always come sailing to your rescue as though I've just dropped by. Simple really, isn't it?

Doorbell rings

Off you go. (*She closes the bedroom door behind her*)

Ellen exits to the front door, opens it

Tindall (*off*) Morning, Mrs Stacey . . .

Ellen (*off*) Morning . . .

Tindall enters. He is dressed casually: anorak, open-necked shirt, jersey. He has a cap which he puts in his pocket. Ellen follows

Tindall I hope I'm not disturbing you in the middle of anything. Not cooking lunch, are you?

Ellen No.

Tindall Ah well, never mind . . .

Ellen I'm . . . not really very hungry.

Tindall No, quite. Terrible thing, grief. Plays merry hell with the digestive system.

Ellen Sorry?

Tindall No Liz today then?

Ellen Erm . . .

Tindall I expected to see her rallying round with saucepans and roasting tins and jars of mint sauce . . .

Ellen No. No, she's . . .

Tindall She's what?

Ellen She's . . . not here.

Tindall Are you expecting her?

Ellen No . . . no.

Tindall (*looking at Ellen*) Good. I wanted to see you alone, Mrs Stacey. I've just been having a little chat with the lady on the ground floor. Mrs Richards. Remarkable for her age, isn't she? Bright as a button. (*He notices the pill-box where Liz left it*) She was telling me all about the events of Friday night. How she heard the dog barking and so on . . . how she saw you, in the entrance hall . . . Very pretty.

Ellen Sorry?

Tindall (*picking up the box*) This box. Is it yours?

Ellen Erm . . . yes . . .

Tindall A present from your husband, no doubt.

Ellen Yes . . . (*She goes to take it*)

Tindall Tell me, what does a girl keep in a little box like this?

Ellen Well . . . it's a pill-box, isn't it?

Tindall Ah. Pills. I see.

Ellen But, erm, you don't have to keep anything in it. I mean, it's just to look at, really . . .

Tindall Quite so. Yes, she caught a glimpse of you as you were waiting for the lift. Well, you know how tempting those little spy-holes are in front doors—you have one yourself, I notice. (*He hands back the pill-box; smiles*) A sensible precaution . . . It was about seven o'clock, was it?

Ellen (*seeing that it's pointless to deny it*) Erm . . . yes. Yes, I . . . think so . . .

Tindall There was someone else there too, she seemed to think. A man. A man with a briefcase. She assumed it was your husband. Couldn't be sure, of course. I mean, an old lady looking through one of those fish-eye lenses . . . Well, it leaves a certain room for doubt, doesn't it? Anyway, a little while later the man left again, in a bit of a hurry—or she assumed it was the same man. She saw him from her kitchen window this time and it *was* getting dark by then, as she herself pointed out. Do interrupt me, if you wish, Mrs Stacey—I have rather a habit of waffling on . . . No? Okay, fair enough. Mrs Richards saw a man with a briefcase arrive and she saw a man with a briefcase leave, and she still didn't really think anything of it until the dog started barking and the body was discovered. The body of your husband. Which rather poses the question of who the man with the briefcase might have been . . . (*Small pause*) Perhaps you could have a think about it. See if you can recall who you might have shared the lift with at about seven o'clock on Friday evening . . .

Ellen Erm . . .

Tindall Yes?

Ellen I don't know . . . Maybe he was going to one of the other flats . . .

Tindall Maybe, yes. But, you see, I've already checked with all the other occupants, and they just can't seem to place him. (*He pauses just long enough to see panic begin to set in. She turns away in confusion*) You are the only one who was seen to be with him, Mrs Stacey. Come now. A smartly dressed man, about forty years old . . . Who was he?

Ellen He wasn't anything to do with me . . .

Tindall stares at her, and slowly advances on her. Pause. Ellen is cornered, and knows it

I mean . . . I'd never met him before.

Tindall Where *did* you meet him? In the entrance hall? Or somewhere else?

Ellen No, he . . . I just got talking to him . . .

Tindall Where?

Ellen In the street. Mike and I had had a bit of a . . . well, a bit of a row, about the decorating, and I . . . went out. For a walk.

Tindall And you met this man in the street?

Ellen Yes. I said. I was feeling, well, upset, I suppose, and he asked me if I was all right. I said I was, but he wouldn't leave me alone. He just kept walking along with me. So I . . . came back here.

Tindall And he followed you?

Ellen Yes.

Tindall And came up here in the lift with you—even though your husband was here?

Ellen Yes. He didn't believe I had a husband. He thought I was bluffing.

Tindall So what happened when you got here?

Ellen Well, that was the awkward bit. Mike actually *wasn't* here. He'd gone to the pub or something . . .

Tindall I see. Do sit down, Mrs Stacey . . .

Ellen (*perching on the sofa*) So, this man started, you know, pawing me and things, and . . . and I kept telling him to stop.

Tindall And did he?

Ellen Well, eventually, yes.

Tindall Then what?

Ellen Then I got him out of the flat and . . . I went off to see Jean . . .

Tindall (*leaning over the sofa*) So why the big denials, Mrs Stacey? If, as you say, you were followed by a strange man but managed to get rid of him, what is there for you to hide? Far more likely, I'd have thought, that you deliberately picked the man up——

Ellen No . . .
Tindall You were angry with Mike—you wanted to get your own back—and you knew he'd be nipping off to the pub. What could be simpler?
Ellen No, it wasn't like that . . .
Tindall Are you sure?

Pause. Ellen now doesn't know which story is more credible

Put it this way. If you want me to believe that this man, whoever he was, had nothing to do with your husband's death, then a little extra-marital hanky-panky is a far more convincing excuse. So. Do you want me to believe you—or not?
Ellen Well, yes, but——
Tindall Good. Hanky-panky it is then. I believe you. (*He smiles, and sits*)

Ellen's nervousness is increasing as she realizes she is being manipulated by him

Don't be frightened, Ellen. Are you frightened of me? You mustn't believe all the stories you hear about policemen, you know. Some of us are really quite human. Comfy sofa, this . . .
Ellen Where's the Sergeant today? Isn't he usually with you?
Tindall Day off. Very religious is Sergeant Goss. So. I have no Sergeant; you have no Liz . . . They are both . . . off-duty. (*Pause*) Unless, of course, she turns up unexpectedly . . .
Ellen Well . . . she might, I suppose. (*She rises, moves towards the hall*) She does sort of drop in without warning . . .
Tindall Very inconsiderate. If I were you I'd put a stop to that.

Taking her cue, Liz quietly opens the bedroom door

Ellen How?
Tindall By bolting the front door, for instance. (*He strides towards the hall in order to do so*)

Liz jumps back inside the bedroom

Ellen No, please! Please don't do that!

Tindall stops

I'm sorry . . . it makes me nervous if I'm locked in . . .
Tindall Ah well. We can't have you feeling nervous. I want you to relax, Ellen. (*He returns, nonchalantly*) I'm sure this whole business can be resolved very easily, if we put our minds to it. This little chat we've been having . . . think of it as off the record. Think of it as a . . . what shall we say? A basis for negotiation.

Ellen gives him a stricken look

Nice curtains, by the way. Oh—were you going to offer me a drink? Now that *is* kind. A small Scotch would be most welcome.

Ellen is by the drinks trolley. She pours Tindall a Scotch. Meanwhile Liz decides she has to try to leave. She edges her way out of the bedroom towards the front door

Ellen Here.
Tindall Aren't you having one?

Reluctantly, Ellen pours a very small drink for herself

Liz opens the front door

What's that noise?
Ellen I didn't hear anything . . .

Tindall goes into the hall again. Nothing. Liz has made her exit. Tindall swiftly opens the door into the bedroom

No—don't go in there . . .

Tindall is already looking around the bedroom and behind the door. He reappears in the hall doorway

Tindall Well well. For a moment then I thought we weren't alone. But it seems we are. (*He approaches her*) Now, I just want you to relax and be co-operative, Ellen. It's in all our interests for you to be co-operative. Do you understand me?

Small pause. Ellen stares at him in open fear. He gives a quiet laugh

Cheers.

Black-out

Scene 2

Monday. About 2 p.m.

Liz is sitting at the table eating yoghurt from a glass dish. She has a glass of white wine, and there is some classical music (perhaps a Chopin étude) playing on the stereo system. It is a very civilized scene

The music finishes, Liz touches the corners of her mouth with a napkin, rises, turns the cassette over, sits down again

Ellen comes out of the bedroom into the living room. She finds her cigarettes

Ellen I don't know how you can carry on eating at a time like this, I really don't . . .
Liz Ellen, anyone would think I was trying to poison you, judging by the way you spurn my cooking. Or perhaps it's something deeper than that: perhaps you find it difficult to accept the favours of your husband's ex-wife . . .
Ellen I've never given a damn about you being his ex-wife.
Liz Good. Women should never let a mere man come between them.

Ellen lights a cigarette

You really ought to give up smoking, you know. Smoking is no longer socially acceptable.

Ellen You think I'm common, don't you? Just because I'm not all worldly like you, just because I don't like fancy curtains and fancy music——

Liz Ellen dear, I don't know why you're in such a rage with me——

Ellen Oh, you don't? Well, perhaps it has something to do with sneaking off yesterday. "I'll just be in the bedroom, so I can pop out and rescue you" she says ... Yeh, thanks a bunch.

Liz Ellen, you really are a complete amateur at all this, aren't you? You honestly expect me to come and interrupt when we're being given a heaven-sent opportunity?

Ellen Heaven-sent? Tindall?

Liz Yes. If only you'd have the wit to see it. I hope you did, Ellen ... (*She clears the dish and glass etc into the kitchen*)

Ellen Hope I did *what*?

Liz Have the wit to use the opportunity.

Ellen You mean sleep with him?

Liz Whatever ...

Ellen Oh, thanks. You think I'm a tart as well, do you?

Liz What I think, Ellen, is of no consequence. Nor what Mike thinks. What *is* of consequence is what Tindall thinks—and if he can't be fooled over this little scheme, then he has to be won over. Right? (*She comes out of the kitchen*) For goodness' sake, girl, we're not concerned with your provincial little morals—this is murder we're talking about!

Ellen Well, I'm sorry, but I'm not going to be bargained over like a piece of meat! In any case, it didn't come to that ...

Liz Didn't it?

Ellen No. He was just testing me. Just seeing if I would ...

Liz (*smiling*) Ellen, that's what men always do. It allows their egos room to breathe if you turn them down.

Ellen You've got an answer for everything, haven't you?

Liz I hope so. On which note, perhaps we ought to discuss arrangements regarding the money ... Now then, in due course, when all the enquiries have led nowhere, you will receive a cheque from the insurance company. You will take it to the bank and cash it. There. Not too taxing a notion, is it?

Ellen And how much do you expect me to hand over to you?

Liz Well, I had anticipated letting you keep, say, thirty thousand.

Ellen Thirty thousand! Out of a hundred and seventy!

Liz All right, forty then. But remember it's not only the price of silence you're paying; it's the price of *collusion* as well.

Ellen You seriously expect me to hand over a hundred and thirty thousand pounds? To you?

Liz Cheap at the price, really. It includes both moral and active support, not to mention the housekeeping.

Ellen My God ... You're incredible ...

Liz Thank you.

Ellen (*bitterly, grinding out her cigarette*) And what about Mike? What does he get?

Liz Are you still concerned about that toe-rag? You might've been dead by now because of him. He's used you, Ellen. Betrayed you.
Ellen You don't know that!
Liz All right, it's an informed guess. A well-informed, from-bitter-experience guess.

The door intercom buzzes. Ellen jumps, involuntarily

Ellen Oh my God ...
Liz And that, if I am not much mistaken, will be the dynamic duo.

Liz holds the receiver out for Ellen

Ellen Hello? Yes. Yes, okay ... (*She presses the intercom button*)
Liz Well done.
Ellen I know what you're doing—you're just trying to get your own back. You're trying to turn me against Mike ...
Liz (*laughing*) Ellen, Mike's done enough things in one lifetime to turn an army of wives against him. And mothers. And mistresses, for that matter. It's a miracle he hasn't been behind bars for years already. He's got a charmed life, that one.
Ellen Then why do you still hang around? Eh? You answer me that!
Liz (*after the briefest of pauses*) Because I need him. Not for what you need him for, but I need him all the same.

The lift is heard, off

Ellen Oh ... you mean ...
Liz (*she jangles her bracelet*) Yes, sweetheart. For the ease and comfort of my weary soul, and the lightening of my despair. As the poet once said.
Ellen What poet?
Liz I don't know ... Any bloody poet.

The doorbell rings

Liz goes into the hall and opens the door

(*Off*) Mr Tindall. How nice.
Tindall (*off*) Afternoon ...

The door closes

Liz and Tindall enter

Liz All alone today? Alone and palely loitering?
Tindall I beg your pardon?
Liz Keats.

Tindall looks blank

Ellen and I were just discussing poets. "O what can ail thee, Knight at arms?" You know the one.
Tindall Not my subject, I'm afraid. I prefer novels. (*To Ellen*) Afternoon, Mrs Stacey.
Liz Detective novels?

Tindall No. Westerns, actually.

Liz Oh, cowboys and Indians. Of *course* . . .

Ellen (*with spirit*) When can I have my husband back, Inspector?

Tindall Soon, Mrs Stacey. The Coroner will be holding a preliminary hearing tomorrow. This is for formal identification purposes only. Then, all being well, the deceased's body will be released for burial or cremation, and the inquest will take place in due course. Now, there are one or two things we still have to discuss, aren't there?

Ellen If you say so.

Tindall First things first. So far we have been working on the assumption that the fatal injuries were caused by the fall from this window, but I've had my doubts about that. And now the post mortem has confirmed my doubts.

Liz Would you care for a cup of coffee, Inspector? I was just about to serve some. Colombian . . .

Tindall No, thank you.

Liz Oh well, just the two of us then. Excuse me. (*She goes to the kitchen*)

Tindall It's a question of the good old blunt instrument, I'm afraid. Has an old-fashioned ring to it, that phrase, doesn't it? The stock-in-trade of many a crime writer. Do you read crime fiction, Mrs Stacey, or do you stick to the excitements of poetry?

Ellen No . . . I . . .

Liz is busy in the kitchen with the coffee, which has been filtering

Liz Ellen finds the women's magazines quite exciting enough, Inspector. She is, in the words of another well-worn phrase, of a nervous disposition. In case you hadn't noticed.

Tindall Oh, I'd noticed that . . .

Ellen How do you know it was a blunt instrument? (*She is making a brave attempt at sounding matter-of-fact*)

Liz enters with the coffee tray

Liz Yes, I'd like to know that too.

Tindall The wounds were not wholly consistent with the impact caused by a fall. Also, minute specks of rust were discovered embedded in the skull tissue . . . Is this too much for you, Mrs Stacey?

Liz We did ask, I'm afraid. Are you all right, Ellen?

Ellen Yes. Yes.

Liz Sugar?

Ellen nods her head. Liz gives her a cup of coffee with sugar

Tindall So, the question is where the rust might have come from . . .

The intercom buzzes

Excuse me. (*At intercom*) Yes. Okay. (*He presses the button*) Both rubbish containers were pushed well back and it was a clear drop all the way. Also there was no trace of blood or tissue on either of them. So it can't have been them.

Liz It's not up to us to find the answers, is it? That's your job.

Tindall Then let me say that in the opinion of the pathologist, the deceased was struck with a heavy metal object before being pushed out of the window. There was no trace of any drug in the body, which implies that the killing was dependent on the element of surprise ...

Ellen and Liz exchange glances. Tindall notes this. Liz, aware of his gaze, goes on the offensive

The lift is heard, outside

Liz Are you certain of all this?

Tindall As I say, it's an opinion. An expert one, however, based on the findings of the post mortem.

Liz Is it possible, then, to distinguish between types of wound when such—forgive me, Ellen—when such extensive damage is done?

Tindall In some cases, yes. For instance, if a body is lying face down, it would be unusual for there to be substantial wounding to the side of the head as well. Even from a height of forty or fifty feet a body doesn't land one way, bounce up again, twist round, and then land another way, inflicting almost equal damage at both points of impact.

The doorbell rings

That'll be Sergeant Goss. (*Lightly*) Perhaps you two ladies would like to have a think about that while I let him in ... (*He goes into the hall*)

Ellen He knows, Liz! He knows everything!

Liz Oh, far from it, Ellen. He's been lucky, that's all.

Ellen Lucky? Jesus! And what about all that stuff about extensive damage? You're not supposed to have seen the body, are you?

Liz Oh, that's a natural assumption, for goodness' sake ... Nobody falls out of a window *without* doing extensive damage.

Ellen We're not going to get away with this—you realize that, don't you?

Liz Pull yourself together, Ellen. The fun's only just beginning ...

Tindall enters, followed by Goss

Sergeant Goss, how very nice to see you ...

Goss Good afternoon.

Tindall Now to the next item on the agenda. The identity of the man in the lift. Sergeant Goss has a *theory* about that ...

Liz (*by the tray*) Coffee, Sergeant?

Goss Oh—that would be very nice. Thank you.

Tindall It's the proper stuff, Gossy.

Goss Ah. Well. Perhaps not this time, thank you.

Tindall And there are no biscuits either, so get on with it.

Goss Right. Well, in the course of checking up on Mr Stacey's insurance position on Saturday, I happened to have a chat with one of the assessors for his old firm, Bradwell Clark and Co ...

Tindall Yes, all right, Gossy, don't spin it out. Get to the point, will you?

Goss I'm at the point. I have just reached it.

Tindall Beg your pardon ...

Goss Which led me to a certain Mr Alan Leathwaite Fisher.

Goss and Tindall watch Ellen and Liz for any sign of reaction. Ellen keeps herself under control, just

Alan Fisher had been given a managerial position, but left shortly after Mike Stacey in order to set up in business on his own. He now has a controlling interest in Argyle Financial Services Ltd, based in Clapham Old Town. He is one of only two former colleagues still in the London area, so I went to see him this morning. And I discovered that Mr Fisher had apparently sent his firm a telegram over this last weekend to the effect that he had been called abroad owing to the sudden illness of his mother. (*He produces it from his jacket pocket*) This is it.

Goss pauses. There is an awkward silence. Tindall paces, slowly

Tindall Go on, Gossy.
Goss Well, the interesting part is that Mr Fisher then turned up for work.

Ellen gives an involuntary gasp. She is becoming very twitchy

Liz Remarkable.
Goss Yes. And he was most surprised to hear about the telegram. Even shocked, according to one of the secretaries. So I made further enquiries, and I've just come from the Telecom office which handled the telegram—sorry, telemessage, they call it now. The message was dictated from a payphone last Friday evening.
Ellen But it can't ... (*She stops herself*)
Tindall You were saying, Mrs Stacey?
Ellen Nothing. Just ... it can't, erm ...
Liz (*swiftly*) It can't be of any great interest to us. And I agree. It's all very intriguing, but why you have to regale us with your minor exploits, Sergeant, I really can't fathom.
Goss Well, you see, we believe there's a connection. A connection between Mr Fisher and Mr Stacey which extends beyond their time at Bradwell Clark and Co. What it boils down to is this: either Mr Fisher is lying, or somebody else sent the telemessage in his name. And why, one asks oneself, would anyone do that?
Ellen When did you say this message was sent?
Goss Last Friday.
Ellen What time?
Goss Six forty-five p.m.
Liz Oh, Ellen, really—what does that matter!
Ellen I don't understand ...
Liz Don't worry about it. Now, why don't you go and put the kettle on again. Make some of your vile brew for our visitors ...
Tindall What don't you understand, Mrs Stacey?
Ellen Oh ... nothing. I ... sorry ...

Tindall sits next to Ellen, his manner sympathetic and concerned

Tindall It's been a terrible strain for you these last few days, Mrs Stacey. Believe me, I do know the sort of things you must be feeling.

Ellen is close to panic. She looks wildly at Liz. Under Goss's gaze, Liz is unable to respond

It's a dreadful business, losing someone close to you in totally unexpected circumstances. You loved your husband, didn't you?

Ellen I still do.

Liz reacts nervously to this apparent gaffe. In their own ways, both she and Ellen are trying to calculate their best method of survival, but the tension is beginning to show

Tindall Of course, of course. Death doesn't stop one loving a person—does it, Sergeant?

Goss In many cases it even enhances the way people feel. All kinds of emotions bubble up to the surface, and it can be a painful process restoring one's self-control.

Tindall Exactly.

Goss I have a theory—just a personal theory, mind—that a person learns more about him or herself during a bereavement than at any other time of life . . .

Tindall Yes, Sergeant Goss is quite a psychologist on the quiet. He understands the way the human mind works—don't you, Gossy?

Goss I do my best.

Tindall He's been on a course, you see. Now, this connection between your husband and Alan Fisher . . . How well did they know each other, would you say?

Ellen Know each other?

Tindall Yes.

Ellen Oh, they didn't know each other——

Liz Ellen, you don't have to say anything! Can't you see they're trying to trick you?

Goss Funny business about that telemessage. One of the secretaries was telling me all about it. In he walked, calm as you please . . .

Ellen It might not have been him.

Tindall Oh, I don't think there was any error there, Mrs Stacey. I mean, an officeful of people can't all be mistaken. Stands to reason, doesn't it?

Ellen But it can't have been him!

Tindall (*casually*) Oh? And why's that?

Liz That's enough, Ellen!

Tindall What makes you say that, Ellen, hm?

Ellen Because . . . because he's . . .

Liz Because he's abroad with his mother. He can't be in two places at once. Simple.

Ellen finally breaks down

Ellen No! He's dead! Alan Fisher is dead. It's no use pretending any more! He's dead . . .

Liz I don't know what's got into you, Ellen. You're obviously quite hysterical.

Tindall How did he die?

Ellen It was him who, you know ... fell out of the window ... It was him.

Tindall And how did he come to be here? (*Small pause*) You brought him, didn't you, Ellen? He was the man in the lift, wasn't he? (*Forcefully*) Wasn't he, Ellen?

Ellen Yes, yes!

Tindall So why did you bring him here? Was it to get your own back on Mike, or was it for some other reason?

Ellen Well, yes, I ... I thought Mike would want to talk to him ...

Tindall Talk to him? About what?

Ellen About, I don't know, pension plans and things ... He'd been saying we ought to be thinking about the future and so on ...

Tindall Yet you claimed on Saturday that you never discussed these matters with your husband, that he always dealt with them.

Ellen Well, yes. He mentioned it in passing, that's all. We never *discussed* it ...

Tindall Yesterday you said you met him in the street—where did you really meet him?

Ellen I ... was in a wine bar ...

Tindall A wine bar? Oh, it's a wine bar now, is it? And you were in there on your own, were you?

Ellen Yes. I'd been to this place once, maybe twice before, though, with Jean ...

Tindall So why did you go on your own last Friday, *before* meeting your friend Jean?

Ellen I don't know! I just did! I mean, I just happened to be in the area doing some shopping, and I saw it and I thought I'd pop in. It's not as if I was going into some rough pub, is it?

Tindall All right, so you met Alan Fisher, asked him back here, and during a conversation with your husband he accidentally fell to his death. Is that it?

Ellen No, of course not! Mike wasn't in—he'd gone to the pub like I said—and when he got back and found me with a strange man here, he, well, he was a bit drunk and he went for him ...

Tindall nods to Goss, who goes out into the hall

Tindall Yes. Go on.

Ellen is trying hard to create an air of conviction. Tindall watches her carefully

Ellen Well. They ... you know ... grappled a bit. And the window was wide open because of the decorating, and Alan Fisher sort of fell against the window sill, and Mike ... well, he picked up a big tin of paint and swung it round, in the heat of the moment, you know ... and ... it hit him, on the side of the head ...

Tindall A tin of paint?

Ellen Yes ... And he ... well, he just sort of fell backwards ... out of the window ...

Tindall But you later identified the body as that of your husband.

Ellen Yes, well, I had to say that, didn't I!

Tindall Why?

Ellen Because . . . because otherwise it would have been murder, wouldn't it? I had to make out it was an accident . . .

Tindall And it would have been difficult to believe that a chance visitor had downed his brief-case and pitched in with a bit of gloss work. Quite. I do see your point. Then there's the painting overalls. They floated down after him, did they, and miraculously fastened themselves around a dead body?

Ellen can find nothing to say

And you, Liz—what do you make of all this?

Liz shakes her head in feigned disbelief

You have no comment?

Liz Nothing I could say would remotely help the situation, one way or the other.

Tindall You underestimate yourself. (*He calls, off*) All right, Sergeant. Bring him in. And tell the helmets to wait.

Fisher enters, escorted by Goss. He is patently the same man we saw with Ellen

Ellen is appalled, incredulous

Ellen But you can't . . . you can't be . . .

Tindall I assure you he can, Ellen. He is, as you can see, very far from being a nasty mess in your backyard.

Ellen But there was a body! There was!

Tindall There was indeed.

Silence

Ellen Oh no . . . no . . . it's not true . . . not Mike . . . (*She seems to react almost in slow motion. Her legs give way and she crumples up on the sofa, giving a series of subdued wails*)

Tindall nods to Goss again

Goss takes Fisher out through the hall

Goss (*indistinctly, off*) Stay put, okay? And don't lose him. We haven't finished with him yet.

Tindall What we have here is a woman who finally discovers that she has been telling the truth. A sorry sight.

Goss enters

Goss All right, Jack, all right . . .

Tindall All this time, thinking she was getting away with an elaborate lie, she has finally woken up to the fact that it wasn't a lie at all. Now there's an intriguing possibility—someone guilty of telling the truth. What do you make of that? Very paradoxical . . .

Goss (*aside*) What's got into you?

Tindall (*snapping*) Take her away, Sergeant. Get her into another room and take her statement.

Goss gives Tindall a long look, then solicitously takes Ellen's arm and leads her into the kitchen

Tindall is alone with the still silent Liz

I'm tired, that's the real truth of all this. Tired of the whole business. Deception. Stupidity. A different motive for each day of the week; a different layer of reality whichever way you turn. I've been a policeman for too long, and it's beginning to get to me . . .

Liz You fancy her, that's your trouble, Jack.

Tindall (*looking at her*) Is that so?

Liz You fancy Ellen . . . But you can have me.

Tindall Ah. Bribery.

Liz Here we both are, thrown together by circumstance. And you know something, there's still a little voice in the back of your head that says Liz Stacey could be a murderer. Isn't there? You think: she's a cool customer; she knows what she's about; she's just the type who could be a party to murder. Don't you? Admit it.

Tindall shrugs and smiles

Have you ever made love to a murder suspect?

Tindall I can't say that I have . . .

Liz Perhaps you ought. It might give you back your taste for police work.

Tindall No. It would just give me back my taste for making love.

Liz Ah, poor divorced thing. No-one suitable at the Singles Club, then?

Tindall Don't mock me, Liz.

Liz moves closer to him. He turns to face her

Liz That's better. I prefer talking to your face. It's more encouraging.

Tindall I am not going to encourage you.

Liz Of course. I forgot you were the scrupulous professional . . . (*She smiles*) You could have me, here, now, right now, if you wanted to . . . (*A beat*) All right, perhaps not. But admit you're intrigued, at least . . .

Tindall stares at her. He reaches out, touches her, as if testing her sincerity, then takes his hand away

Tindall You like to live dangerously . . .

Liz Oh, you remembered . . . Yes. Life is wasted on the faint-hearted, I've always felt.

Tindall I knew someone else like you once. Someone who liked to push each situation to the extreme . . .

Liz Who was that? (*A smile*) Your wife?

Tindall (*not smiling*) No. A colleague of mine.

Liz Tell me more.

Tindall He made Chief Super, and then got done for corruption. But of course you'd know about all that, wouldn't you?

Brief pause. Liz then gives another warm smile, relaxes

Liz I like you, Inspector. (*She leans in and kisses him*)

Tindall forces himself away, holds her at arms' length, but this is neither an immediate nor an instinctive reaction

Tindall The more you play up to me, the more reason you must have for doing so—that's the only conclusion that I, a cynical copper, can draw from this.
Liz I wouldn't expect anything else.
Tindall Tell me: did you know Mike Stacey was dead?
Liz Well, yes . . . That's what you said the night it happened. And there was no reason to doubt it . . .

They are now both thinking on their feet, disguising their battle of wits as mere conversation

Tindall But Ellen genuinely believed Mike was still alive, I'm convinced of that, even though she saw the body . . . Of course, she was assuming it was Fisher, and being a bit squeamish she probably didn't want to look too closely at the remains . . . (*He paces slowly, thinking it out*) Suppose Fisher was blackmailing Mike . . . And suppose Mike runs out of money to pay him off . . . Isn't it possible that Fisher used Ellen to get rid of Mike and claim his life insurance instead?
Liz What, have an affair with her simply to get at Mike?
Tindall A two-pronged attack, yes. His money and his wife. What do you think?
Liz I think you're clutching at straws.
Tindall Maybe. But if Ellen conspired with Fisher to murder Mike, why was she so shocked to see Fisher alive? And if she conspired with *Mike* to murder *Fisher* . . . how did the plan misfire?
Liz I have no idea. Look, perhaps she genuinely brought a man back here, knowing that Mike would be down at the boozer by then . . . Has that possibility remotely crossed your mind?
Tindall Oh, indeed it has. (*Pause*) And you—what do you stand to gain from all this?
Liz Gain? Why should I gain anything?
Tindall Oh, come on, Liz. You're no philanthropist. What's in it for you?

Brief pause

Liz Very well. The way I look at it is: everyone should get their just deserts. And I mean everyone . . . After all, that's what insurance is all about, isn't it? It provides for us in the event of a crisis. And who knows, Inspector, you too might one day face a crisis . . .
Tindall Are you saying what I think you're saying?
Liz It's a tough old world. And we're none of us getting any younger. Or richer. Whereas insurance companies are insured to make sure they get richer . . . A nice simple verdict of accidental death would work wonders with even the most tight-fisted of them, I'm sure . . .

Tindall You *are* saying what I think you're saying . . .
Liz (*smiling*) A hundred and seventy thousand goes a long way, Jack. Then there's the double indemnity clause, in case of *accidental* death. Three hundred and forty thousand. Not to be sneezed at. And what kind of pension can *you* look forward to? (*A small pause*) What have you got to lose? Your career prospects, your marriage—they're already up the spout anyway.
Tindall Thanks for reminding me.
Liz Close the case. Forget plots; forget Fisher. You have one dead body, indisputably that of Mike Stacey. Stick to the basic facts, and there's no hard evidence to disprove any of it. (*Brief pause*) All you have to do is say the word, and lives can change. Yours. Mine. Ellen's. See? You have a magic wand. All you have to do is wave it.

Tindall appears to consider for a second or two. Liz looks at him intently, the gleam of triumph in her eye. He smiles at her

You won't regret it, Jack. (*She gives him another kiss*)

Black-out

SCENE 3

A short while later

Liz and Fisher are sitting, separately. Tindall is standing. Goss is bringing Ellen back into the room from the kitchen

Tindall Please sit down, Mrs Stacey.

Ellen does so

Now, there's a series of known facts in this case—fact number one: we have a dead body, that of Michael Dennis Stacey. Fact number two: according to both Forensic and the pathologist he was killed by a blow to the head before being discovered in the back yard. (*To Ellen*) A blow which would have left the paintpot somewhat dented to say the least, Mrs Stacey. Needless to say, it was not. Fact number three——

Liz is beginning to realize that her efforts have failed and that Tindall is not going to play it her way

Liz Inspector, are you sure you wish to pursue all this? Is it *worth* it?
Tindall I'm no fairy godmother, Liz. I'm too old to believe in magic wands. (*Resuming*) Fact number three: (*he clicks his fingers*) a document.

Goss produces the document

Do you recognize it, Mr Fisher?
Fisher (*casually*) Yes.
Goss Could you tell us what it is?
Fisher (*giving Goss a withering look*) It's an application form for a personal pension plan.

Tindall Very good. (*He indicates under the sofa*) I found it here.
Liz (*aside, fiercely*) Don't do this, Jack. What does it achieve?
Tindall We'll see, won't we? So, Mr Fisher, I take it you're not going to deny being here on Friday evening?
Fisher No.
Tindall And what was your reason for being here?
Fisher I was invited. By Mrs Stacey.
Tindall For what purpose?
Fisher Supposedly to discuss certain professional matters with her husband.
Tindall And did you do that?
Fisher No.
Tindall Why not?
Fisher He wasn't here.
Tindall So what did you do?
Fisher I talked to Mrs Stacey instead.
Tindall About pension plans?
Fisher Amongst other things . . .
Tindall And then what?

Ellen glares at Tindall. He continues, smoothly

Fisher I had a drink and left.
Ellen Liar!

Ellen makes to get up, but Liz restrains her

Tindall You knew Mike Stacey, didn't you?
Fisher More knew *of* him, than knew him . . .
Tindall You used to work together.
Fisher We worked for the same firm for a while, yes.
Tindall So why on earth would he want advice from an ex-colleague on matters he already knew backwards?
Fisher I don't know. (*Brief pause*) I didn't know it was him when I met Mrs Stacey.
Tindall In the wine bar, you mean?
Fisher That's right. I didn't connect the name.
Tindall And when did you connect the name?
Fisher After I got here.
Tindall You mean you recognized the flat?
Fisher No. He wasn't living here when I knew him. And he wasn't married to this Mrs Stacey either.
Tindall I see. So you had no idea who Ellen Stacey was—nor who her husband was?
Fisher No. I said. I only knew it was him when I saw that photo of him. (*He indicates a small framed photograph of Mike and Ellen*)
Tindall And why do you suppose someone should send a telegram saying you'd be away from the office?
Fisher I have no idea.
Tindall No idea at all?
Fisher People do funny things.

Tindall Ah, you mean practical jokes, that sort of thing . . .

Fisher Yes. I suppose.

Tindall And why should anyone play a practical joke like that?

Fisher I've told you: I don't know! There are some weird people around!

Tindall Oh indeed there are, Mr Fisher. (*He turns to Ellen*) Now, Mrs Stacey, perhaps you can tell us why you drugged Mr Fisher's drink on Friday evening, after you'd invited him back here . . .

Ellen What?

Tindall That is what you did, isn't it? Or did you rely merely on your female charms to render him insensible?

Ellen I . . .

Tindall Yes?

Ellen Well, I . . .

Tindall I'll tell you something, Mrs Stacey: I'm sick and tired of all the little games you and your friend Liz have been indulging in for the last few days. I've a pretty shrewd idea as to what actually happened, and you are going to help me prove it. (*Forcefully*) Now answer the question!

Ellen (*hopelessly*) Yes, I . . . put something in his drink. Or I thought I did . . .

Tindall For what purpose exactly?

Ellen (*shrugs*) To make him unconscious . . .

Tindall Why? So Mike Stacey could kill him?

Ellen Yes.

Liz Ellen, he can't bully you into a confession, you know.

Tindall (*viciously*) You! Shut it!

Liz She has the right to remain silent.

Tindall Don't tell me my job!

Goss Jack . . . ease off, will you? Don't spoil it now . . .

Tindall Spoil it? Spoil it? What the hell are you on about? Fall over backwards and let them walk all over you, you would, just because they're women.

Goss Oh, for God's sake . . .

Tindall That's why you are what you are, Gossy. You've got no instinct about killers at all! You're soft . . .

Liz Boys, boys . . . please.

Goss Yes, I'm sorry, Mrs Stacey . . .

Tindall grabs Goss by his jacket

Tindall Don't you ever apologize for me. Do you hear? Sergeant?

Goss (*as calmly as he can manage*) Would you like me to continue this investigation, sir? You're obviously not feeling up to it at the moment.

Tindall (*levelly*) Get lost, Gossy. (*He releases him. To Ellen*) Mrs Stacey, is it or is it not true that with your husband Mike Stacey you plotted to kill Alan Fisher in order to claim life insurance, fraudulently, on your husband's policy?

A slight pause. Then Ellen nods

Liz Ellen——

Ellen It's no use, Liz.

Tindall And is it or is it not true that this plan backfired and your husband was killed instead?

Ellen (*to Fisher*) How the hell did you do it! You collapsed—I saw you!

Tindall Thank you. Mr Fisher, were you or were you not rendered unconscious by the drink Mrs Stacey gave you?

Fisher Not to my knowledge.

Tindall Not to your knowledge?

Unsettled now, Fisher begins to vacillate

Fisher Well, that is, I suppose I might have been, but I have no recollection . . .

Tindall What you mean is: no, you weren't, but if it helps to clear you of murder then you won't deny it—is that right? Hm? Is it?

Fisher I . . . well . . . no, like I say, I have no recollection of collapsing, but now you mention it I suppose I could have passed out for, I don't know, five minutes or so . . .

Tindall Without realizing it?

Fisher Yes. It can happen, Inspector.

Tindall Mr Fisher, I suggest you didn't pass out at all, although you knew that Mrs Stacey would attempt to make you do so.

Ellen What . . .?

Fisher I don't follow you.

Tindall I suggest that your visit here on Friday evening was no accident. You *knew* Mrs Stacey would meet you in the wine bar, and you knew she would ask you back here on the pretext of talking to her husband.

Ellen No, no, this is crazy . . .

Tindall You also knew, Mr Fisher, that she was planning to set you up, and you pretended to pass out, having carefully managed *not* to drink anything—what was it, the old tipping it in the flowerpot routine? Or is that too much of a cliché for someone as subtle as you?

Ellen is both riveted and appalled by this turn of events

Perhaps you prefer the wads of super-absorbent Kleenex or the endless supply of handkerchiefs?

Fisher You know something—your Sergeant here is right. You're way out of line, Mr Tindall, and I'm getting rather pissed off with your whole manner and the way you're conducting this investigation. We don't have to stand here and listen to your ravings. If you want to use us as punchbags for your own warped little ego, fine, but I want a solicitor present.

Tindall As soon as you are charged you will have that right.

Fisher Oh, so you're going to charge me, are you? What with? Just what the hell do you think you can prove against me?

Tindall I think I can prove that you committed a premeditated murder.

Fisher gives a snort of disdain

Fisher Seems to me you ought to be taken off this case, Tindall. It seems to me you've let your private problems cloud your judgement.

Small pause. Tindall watches him, bides his time. Fisher, however, senses he has struck home and gains confidence

Oh, I know what you're at—you think you can regain your reputation by pulling in a good result. You've got it in for all of us, haven't you? Even poor old Sergeant Goss. How do we know what you say about this case is true? You spout on about forensic this and post mortem that—it could all be a load of bull as far as we know. This could be a simple case of accidental death, exactly as it looked, but you're so determined to be a hero you'll do anything to turn it into murder!

Tindall Sergeant Goss will corroborate all the evidence, Mr Fisher. Forensic or otherwise.

Fisher Will you, Sergeant? Have you seen the lab reports? Have you actually seen the results of the post mortem?

Goss Yes, I've seen them.

Fisher You've seen bits of paper in Tindall's hand, maybe, but have you actually read them yourself?

Goss No, but——

Fisher Right. So ask yourself about the Inspector's motives. It's always the suspects who are supposed to have all the *motives*, isn't it? But what about the police? Ask yourself what he'd stand to gain if he pulled this one out of the hat.

Goss gives Tindall a wary look, but says nothing

Tindall Yes, yes, yes, very good, Mr Fisher. Very eloquent. But you fail to take account of one rather important detail: Mrs Stacey has admitted that she plotted to kill you.

Fisher But I'm here, Inspector. I'm alive.

Tindall Her husband isn't.

Fisher So he fell out of the window. OK, OK, maybe Ellen and Mike *planned* something, maybe they did, but it didn't happen, did it? I am the proof of that. We can all plan things, Mr Tindall—I can plan to rob the Bank of England, but I'm not guilty of anything until I actually do it.

Goss That's not strictly true, in point of fact . . .

Fisher Anyway, who's to say Ellen and Mike didn't quarrel, and Ellen shoved him off the ledge herself?

Ellen You what?

Fisher Or maybe the silly bugger was showing off—trying to scare Ellen. I wouldn't have put that past him either.

Ellen How dare you say that? How dare you say I did it? You're the one who killed him, not me. I wasn't *there*!

Fisher Then how can you know what happened?

Ellen, about to retaliate, is wrong-footed by this

A point to me, I think. However, I can see I haven't convinced you, Inspector. But the Sergeant now . . . You're thinking twice, aren't you, Sergeant?

Goss I . . . don't know what to think . . .

Tindall God, you're a prat, Gossy. He's just playing for time.

Goss And the evidence?

Tindall (*contemptuously*) All genuine. You can check it back at the station.

Fisher There's one thing you can't check, Sergeant.

Tindall And what's that?

Fisher The murder weapon. If, as you say, Inspector, Mike Stacey was hit over the head before being dumped out of the window—what was he hit with?

Pause. They all wait for a response from Tindall

You yourself have ruled out the can of paint, and, correct me if I'm wrong, but I'd have thought it's much more difficult to prove a murder case without a murder weapon.

Tindall I have my ideas about the weapon.

Fisher Your ideas ... You're all washed up as a policeman, Tindall, and you know it. Be realistic; if your superiors really thought this was a murder case they wouldn't have let a wideboy like you loose on it, would they? (*Slight pause*) See? Look at him. Look at him, Sergeant. He's cracking up. He threw away his chances of promotion when he was in the Drugs Squad—took the stuff himself, I shouldn't wonder ...

Tindall I think you've said enough, Mr Fisher.

Fisher Getting a bit near the knuckle, am I? And of course you know all about knuckles, don't you? Perhaps you'd like to have a go at *me*, Inspector? Go on. It wouldn't be the first time you've got a bit rough with somebody, would it?

This is what Tindall has been waiting for

Tindall Is that so?

Fisher So I hear.

Tindall And *where* might you have heard all this, Mr Fisher? On the nine o'clock news?

Fisher Hardly.

Tindall Then where?

Fisher Oh, around. You know ...

Tindall Bit of gossip down the local boozer, was it? Or do you also have a friend who's very "pally" with my ex-Chief Superintendent? Eh?

Fisher I don't know what you're getting at ... (*His bravado is beginning to evaporate*)

Tindall Oh, don't you? Well, what I'm getting at, Mr Fisher, is that you are not the only one who's claiming inside knowledge about my supposedly thwarted career.

Fisher Really?

Tindall Yes, really. And I find it mighty coincidental that the other highly knowledgeable person is also in this room. You've been very quiet of late, Liz. That's not like you. Has anything been bothering you? Have you been willing Mr Fisher to keep his big mouth shut, by any chance? Cocky bastard, isn't he?

Fisher OK, so Liz Stacey and I have had a chat ... So what? It's a free country.

Tindall Careless talk costs lives, Mr Fisher. To coin a phrase.

Ellen stares at Liz, then at Fisher, the beginnings of understanding stirring in her

Oh, and for your information, I only assault drug pushers. And only when there is a knife being aimed at my neck. (*To Ellen*) Are you all right, Mrs Stacey?

Ellen I ... yes, I ...

Tindall Good. Now, Mr Fisher—you were asking about the murder weapon. I have a feeling the ladies could tell you more about that than I can.

Goss (*perplexed*) The ladies, sir?

Tindall You're not a betting man, are you, Gossy? If you were, I'd bet you fifty quid I'll find the weapon, and I'd bet you another fifty you'd still think I was acting on trumped up evidence.

Goss I'm ... sorry about that, Jack. I admit I did wonder, just for a second ...

Tindall You've got to know whose side you're on, Gossy. No use letting these clever bastards get you rattled. Got a chisel handy?

Goss Eh?

Tindall There's one in the kitchen drawer ...

Goss Kitchen drawer. Right ...

Goss goes into the kitchen

Tindall I think we'll find, Mr Fisher, that if the window still opens smoothly, the weapon will be back in place. Isn't that so, Ellen? Perhaps you would be so kind, Sergeant ...

Goss comes back with the chisel

Goss Sir?

Tindall Open the window.

Goss does so. It rises smoothly. Fisher instinctively moves towards the window

You stay where you are, Mr Fisher. Right, Sergeant, gloves on. Open up the access panel in the frame, would you? (*With emphasis*) That narrow bit, just there ...

Goss takes a pair of protective latex gloves from his pocket, and puts them on. He then works at the frame with the chisel, levering out the slim panel of wood

We have now come to Fact number four: the weapon. You see, the only way all the facts fit is if you were in on the plot too, Mr Fisher. (*To Ellen*) He came here knowing you were planning to kill him, and was able to turn the tables on Mike, who was expecting him to be unconscious. The question is: how did he know about the plan in advance? (*His manner is now almost teasing. He is enjoying this*) I kept thinking that you must be involved with him somehow, Ellen—but I was barking up the wrong tree, wasn't I? It wasn't you at all.

Ellen Then who?

Tindall looks at Liz

Liz?

Goss extracts the sash cord, wedges the frame, and proceeds to untie the weight, which is a heavy, cylindrical lump of iron

Tindall You've got it. Bravo. Still want to take over the investigation, Gossy? O ye of little faith?
Goss Certainly not, sir.
Tindall Take it to Forensic, there's a good chap. I'm sure it's now clean as a whistle, but you never know . . .

Goss puts the weight into a protective bag and places the bag on a shelf. Liz pours herself a whisky

Liz You don't mind if I have a drink, do you? Thank you so much.

During the ensuing dialogue, Liz unfastens her bracelet and unobtrusively empties the heroin into the glass. We see this, Ellen sees it, but no-one else. Liz then stands, casually holding the glass. And we are left waiting to see if, and when, she will drink . . .

Tindall Your husband not only plotted with you, Mrs Stacey, but with his first wife as well, whose untimely arrival on Friday night was all part of their scheme. You would set up Fisher, and Liz would move in on you, presumably cutting you out of the deal to a greater or lesser extent.
Ellen I don't believe this . . .
Tindall Oh, but I think you do, Mrs Stacey. I think it is all beginning to make a very nasty kind of sense. What we weren't clear about till just now was that she also devised her own little plot with Fisher, thereby cutting Mike out of the deal too, in the most effective way possible . . .
Ellen No, no . . .
Tindall (*to Liz's face*) A very generous lady is our Liz: she likes to have an intrigue going with just about everybody . . .

Liz remains impassive, snapping shut the bracelet on her wrist

Understanding the implications of this all too clearly, and not wanting Liz to take the "easy" way out, Ellen goes to her and grabs the glass from her

Ellen Don't you dare!
Liz (*making light of it*) Okay, so it's your whisky. I wasn't really that thirsty anyway . . .

Ellen pours herself a whisky

Tindall Been lovers long, have you, Liz? You and Fisher? I must say, your idea of loyalty would put a Judas to shame.
Liz Oh, Jack, spare us the lofty moralizing, please. It doesn't become you, you know . . .
Tindall As to the telegram—you'd assumed there wouldn't be one, hadn't you? You'd assumed Mike Stacey was going to send it *after* the murder.

Goss Instead of which he sent it from a phone near the wine bar, at a time when Fisher was seen to be there.
Tindall Quite.
Goss A case of retribution already being in the post when the deed was done . . .
Tindall Very poetic, Sergeant. I'm sure the ladies will appreciate that.

Fisher is looking decidedly nervy by now, Liz still remarkably cool

(*To Goss*) All right, do your stuff . . .
Goss Elizabeth Stacey and Ellen Mary Stacey, you are under arrest on a charge of conspiracy to commit murder; Alan Leathwaite Fisher, you are under arrest on a charge of murder. You have the right to remain silent, but anything you do say——

Ellen sways slightly, as if about to faint

Liz Ellen——
Goss Jack—Mrs Stacey's going to faint——

Tindall moves across to support Ellen. Fisher takes the opportunity of this diversion to grab the sash weight from where Goss had placed it. He runs towards the hall

Hey! (*Calling*) McBride! Pearson!

Fisher turns and heads for the window. It is the only other way out. He is brandishing the weight, now free of its bag, in order to keep them at bay

Tindall Don't be insane, Fisher!

Tindall manoeuvres Ellen into an armchair. Fisher gets onto the window-ledge, in a sitting position, looks down, pauses

How many men are down there?
Goss Two at the back; one at the front.
Tindall Right, get Pearson and McBride down there as well. Fast!

Goss runs out into the hall

Goss (*off*) Downstairs, quick. Fisher's on the ledge . . . And radio through for fire and ambulance . . . *Now*.
Fisher We screwed it, Liz . . .
Tindall Well, what's it to be? Throw yourself down there, as they originally intended, or give yourself up and *walk* down with me?

Goss enters

Goss Fire and ambulance are being alerted, sir . . .
Tindall You see? They're coming to take you away, Fisher. It'd make everyone's job a lot easier if they didn't have to scrape you off the concrete first.

Fisher hovers on the ledge, looking up, down, all around, thinking furiously. Tindall takes a step towards him. He lashes out with the weight

Fisher You stay back, Tindall! (*To Liz*) You reckon you'll get off, don't you, Liz? You reckon you'll get out of this scot free!
Liz (*smiling*) The evidence against me is purely circumstantial . . .
Fisher Oh, you made sure of that, didn't you?
Liz One has to prepare for all eventualities, Alan.
Goss Right, come here you——

While Fisher is distracted Goss makes to grab hold of him. In trying to avoid Goss's grasp Fisher slips, and disappears

Jack!

Tindall rushes to the window, and looks out. Goss sinks back into the room. Liz is transfixed, at a loss

Liz Oh good God . . .
Goss I couldn't hold him, Jack. I just couldn't hold him . . .
Tindall All right, Gossy, take it easy . . .

Tindall gives Goss a supportive pat on the shoulder. There is a horrid silence. Tindall then turns his attention back to Ellen, who is sitting motionless

Now, Mrs Stacey . . . are you okay?

There is no reaction from Ellen

Ellen? (*Suddenly worried, he shakes her, looks into her eyes*) Christ, she must have taken something . . .
Liz (*taking in the situation*) Oh no. She saw me do it! She saw me put it in the whisky . . .
Tindall What? Put what?
Liz She thought *I* was going to drink it . . .
Tindall What was it? Heroin?

Liz nods

(*To Goss*) Get that ambulance crew here now!

Goss is already halfway to the front door

Liz She must have done this deliberately . . .
Tindall How the hell do you know that!

Tindall takes off his jacket, puts it round Ellen to keep her warm, feels for her pulse

Liz I could see it in the way she looked at me. She knew what it was . . .
Tindall She poured herself a drink. She probably picked up the wrong bloody glass . . .

There are two glasses where Ellen has put them down, one almost full, the other almost empty. Tindall holds Ellen's head up

Ellen! Ellen, how much did you drink? How much?

Ellen's head slumps forward. He pulls it up, looks into her eyes again

Warm water, quick.

Liz runs to the kitchen, grabs a cup, fills it from the tap

How big was the dose?
Liz (*off*) About three hundred milligrams.
Tindall Jesus . . .
Liz It was for Alan . . . A less painful way out . . .

Liz returns. Tindall tries to make Ellen drink

Tindall Come on, Ellen . . .

Goss comes back

Goss The ambulance is on its way, Jack . . .

Liz sinks to the floor beside Ellen

Liz I didn't intend this . . . Oh, the stupid girl . . .
Tindall A little late in the day for sentiment, isn't it?

Tindall releases Ellen, and stands. Ellen sinks back into the chair

Right. Time to go. Gossy . . .

Liz rises, composes herself, collects her bag, neatly wipes the corner of each eye with a handkerchief. Goss indicates for her to leave

Liz Well. Congratulations, Jack. I'm sure the Chief Super will be proud of you.
Tindall He will be if I get a conviction.
Liz We shall see, shan't we? I look forward to doing battle with you again. (*She goes to the door*) Are you going to handcuff me, Sergeant, or shall we go arm in arm?

Goss, dignified to the last, merely waits. Liz looks back at Ellen, then at Tindall. Their eyes meet

Liz and Goss exit

The ambulance is heard approaching (off). Tindall gently retrieves his jacket, looks at Ellen, and shakes his head ruefully. The lift descends

Tindall then carefully picks up both glasses with a handkerchief, inspects them, replaces them

Tindall (*almost to himself*) What did you hope to achieve, Ellen? You'd have been out in two or three years . . . Had your whole life ahead of you . . . Ah well.

Tindall exits. We hear the front door open and close

The ambulance arrives, below, and the siren cuts out

Just as we expect the lights to fade, Ellen moves. She sits up, looks around. She rises, goes to the window, takes in the scene below, then starts towards the hall door

At the same time, Tindall steps back into the room

With a gasp, Ellen stops in her tracks

Tindall Not very clever, Ellen. A nice try, I admit, but you wouldn't have got further than the South Circular.

Ellen turns away, slumps onto the sofa. Tindall approaches her

Now, let's be co-operative, shall we?

Ellen looks at him in alarm, then edges away

Ellen No! Keep away . . .

Tindall I don't mean that. Well, I do—but I'm not going to let it spoil our relationship. (*He sits next to her*) You're my star witness, Ellen. You're my only chance of getting a result with Liz. So. I'm going to look after you. I'll have to charge you with conspiracy to commit murder, of course, but I might forget about your little attempt just now to pervert the course of justice. And who can say fairer than that? Shall we go? (*He stands, and waits*) It's the best offer you'll get from me, Ellen. (*Brief pause. He then continues, ominously*) Until you're a free woman again, that is.

Ellen looks at him. He offers his arm. She stands and slowly moves to take it

The Lights fade

CURTAIN

FURNITURE AND PROPERTY PLOT

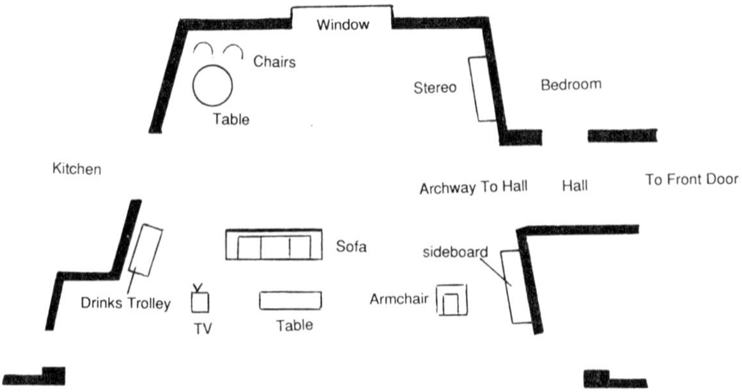

ACT I

Scene 1

On stage: *Kitchen area:*
Fridge
Teapot and cups, etc.
Tray
Filter coffee maker

Living area:
Houseplants
Stereo system
Small TV set
Up-to-date posters and ornaments
Sofa. *Under it:* insurance form
Table
Chairs
Armchairs
Intercom system at hall doorway
Large open sash window. *In it:* iron weight
Drinks trolley. *On it:* bottles and glasses, including whisky, brandy, ginger ale
Telephone
Pocket calculator in drawer
Framed photo of Mike and Ellen
Bundled-up dust sheets
Large tin of gloss paint
Table lamps
Conventional general furnishings

Personal: **Fisher**: briefcase. *In it:* papers

SCENE 2

Set: Magazines, ashtray full of cigarette stubs

Personal: **Liz**: Bag. *In it:* holiday brochures
Ellen: Cigarettes
Goss: watch (used throughout), notebook
Tindall: warrant card

SCENE 3

On stage: As before but dust sheets removed, window closed

Personal: **Liz**: Two bags of shopping. *In one:* milk
Ellen: Watch

ACT II

SCENE 1

On stage: One curtain in place, one off the wall
Stepladder

Personal: **Ellen**: handbag. *In it:* handkerchief, make-up, comb etc, pill box
Liz: heavy silver bracelet with hollow compartment

SCENE 2

Set: *On table:* napkin, glass dish of yoghurt, glass of white wine
Elsewhere: Ellen's cigarettes and lighter

SCENE 3

Off-stage: Chisel

Personal: **Goss**: pair of latex gloves, protective bag
Liz: handbag. *In it:* handkerchief

LIGHTING PLOT

Interior setting. Practical fittings required: table lamps

ACT I, Scene 1

To open: Evening light, beginning to fade

Cue 1 **Ellen** switches on table lamps (Page 1)
Snap on lamps and covering spots

Cue 2 **Fisher** switches bedroom light on and off (Page 4)
Snap bedroom light on and off

Cue 3 **Mike** moves towards Fisher (Page 5)
Black-out

ACT I, Scene 2

To open: Evening. All practicals on

Cue 4 **Goss** switches on main lights (Page 6)
Snap on general lighting

Cue 5 **Ellen** stares blankly ahead (Page 14)
Black-out

ACT I, Scene 3

To open: Afternoon lights. Flicker from TV

Cue 6 **Tindall** switches off TV set (Page 14)
Cut TV flicker

Cue 7 **Ellen** flicks through TV channels (Page 23)
Flicker from TV

Cue 8 **Ellen** gives a wail (Page 32)
Black-out

ACT II, Scene 1

To open: General lighting, morning

Cue 9 **Tindall** gives a quiet laugh (Page 32)
Black-out

ACT II, Scene 2

To open: General lighting. Afternoon

Cue 10 **Liz** kisses Tindall (Page 43)
Black-out

ACT II, Scene 3

To open: General lighting. Afternoon

Cue 11 **Ellen** moves to take Tindall's arm (Page 54)
Fade to black-out

EFFECTS PLOT

Occasional sounds of trains and main road traffic can be heard throughout the action

ACT I

Cue 1 As Curtain rises (Page 1)
Sound of lift

Cue 2 As Scene 3 begins (Page 14)
Sound of old film on TV. Channels changed to race meeting

Cue 3 **Tindall** switches TV off (Page 14)
Snap off TV sound

Cue 4 **Liz**: "... can have it on account." (Page 22)
Sound of lift

Cue 5 **Ellen** flicks through TV channels (Page 23)
Intermittent TV noise

ACT II

Cue 6 **Liz**: "... over the place with a fine toothcomb." (Page 28)
Intercom buzzes

Cue 7 **Liz**: "... for goodness sake." (Page 28)
Sound of lift

Cue 8 **Liz**: "Simple really, isn't it?" (Page 28)
Doorbell

Cue 9 As Scene 2 begins (Page 32)
Classical music from stereo. Cassette ends. Liz turns it over. Music plays again

Cue 10 **Liz**: "... from-bitter-experience guess." (Page 34)
Intercom buzzes

Cue 11 **Liz**: "... I need him all the same." (Page 34)
Sound of lift

Cue 12 **Liz**: "Any bloody poet." (Page 34)
Doorbell

Cue 13 **Tindall**: "... where the rust might have come from." (Page 35)
Intercom buzzes

Cue 14 **Ellen** and **Liz** exchange glances (Page 36)
Sound of lift

Cue 15 **Tindall**: "At both points of impact." (Page 36)
Doorbell

Cue 16	**Liz** and **Goss** exit *Ambulance is heard approaching*	(Page 53)
Cue 17	**Tindall** shakes his head ruefully *Sound of lift*	(Page 53)
Cue 18	**Tindall**: "Ah well." *Ambulance siren stops*	(Page 53)